HIGH-TECH HARASSMENT

HIGH-TECH HARASSMENT

How to Get Even with Anybody Anytime

Scott French

BARRICADE
BOOKS

Fort Lee, New Jersey

Other books by Scott French:

Credit: The Cutting Edge

SpyGame: Winning Through Super Technology (with Lee Lapin)

Never Say Lie: How to Beat the Machines, the Interviews, the
Chemical Tests (with Paul Van Houten, Ph.D)

THANKS TO THE MANY PEOPLE WHO CONTRIBUTED TO THIS PROJECT.
—Scott

Published by Barricade Books Inc.
1530 Palisade Avenue
Fort Lee, New Jersey 07024
by arrangement with Paladin Press

Distributed by Publishers Group West
4065 Hollis
Emeryville, CA 94608

Printed in the United States of America

Library of Congress Cataloging-in-Publication Data

French, Scott R.
   High-tech harassment: how to get even with anyone anytime /
Scott French.
ISBN 0-942637-71-2 : $14.95
1. Revenge—Humor. I. Title.
PN6231.R45F74   1993
818'.5402—dc20   92-36260
                        CIP

0 9 8 7 6 5 4 3 2 1

Neither the author nor the publisher assumes any responsibility
for the use or misuse of information contained in this book.

CONTENTS

TO THE MOTHERS OF AMERICA, I APOLOGIZE

There should be no need for this book. Were you raised in a barn? Don't you ever think of anyone else but yourself? Yes, sir. No, ma'am . . .

It seems so simple, really. The golden rule actually sums it up fairly succinctly. You remember: "Do onto others as . . ."

Do you remember? You'd be surprised at how many people have no idea what the hell I'm talking about.

And that's the problem.

No, sir, I don't mind that you require the sound of MTV at 3:00 in the morning in the apartment next to mine. And God knows since the batteries on your hearing aid died a premature death, you probably have to turn the volume up four notches past the threshold of human pain.

Oh yes, and about your dog. You know the one; that lovely little hairball that sits directly outside my window from 8:00 A.M. on and whines incessantly because xxxx inbreeding has purged any dim memories of survival without a white couch to lay his pretty little head on.

And you know the fact that I work nights and have to try to achieve a semblance of unconsciousness with a pillow clamped over my head to block out the endless howling and crying?

Don't give it a second thought.

Your fat, ugly Japanese sports car parked across my driveway which made me two hours late for work? Not worth troubling yourself over. I didn't want to work in show business anyway, and I know how bad those legs can ache when you have to walk that extra block from the legal parking place.

And what would my precious day off be like if I was forced to sit through a new movie *without* someone like you sitting in the seat next to me dissecting the actor's performance as loudly as possible?

vii

To the lovely creature at the bank who bounced my rent check because my paycheck hadn't "cleared" (regardless of the fact that I have been paying your goddamn service fee for six years for you to "take care" of my money and never so much as wrote a check out of order); to the gentleman who has stuffed my mailbox with bulky, unwanted, and illegal chain-letter schemes that I never asked for; to those friendly folks at the phone company who put their careers ahead of finishing high school (and rightly so, one might add); to the garbagemen (sorry, I mean the "sanitation engineers") who hate to get out of bed at 4:00 in the morning and want to share that unpleasant experience with as many innocent folks as possible; to jerkoffs at airports, on ships, and in restaurants everywhere who think it's up to me to enhance their stock portfolios *without the benefit of service*; and to those "companies" that have forgotten that their customers were the very people who allowed them to have a greater GNP and more power then most third world countries will ever enjoy . . .

To all of you who have forgotten the basic concept that ONE IS RESPONSIBLE FOR ONE'S OWN ACTIONS, I say:

"Just because I'm polite, doesn't mean I'm weak."

REVENGE WITH ÉLAN

There have been numerous famous quotations on the subject of revenge. The one that's most commonly found in revenge manuals, spy books, and a number of sleazy novels is attributed to Confucius: "Revenge is a dish best served cold . . ."

I don't know. That seems kind of lame. I realize Confucius had a limited amount of material to work with, and his scribes probably screwed around with what he said (like editors everywhere, they felt they had to claim a piece of the action), but I still suspect he said something much more solid than that.

No doubt the original wording suffered further as it was cut down to size by underpaid, out-of-work book editors moonlighting at Chinese fortune-cookie factories.

Revenge, in its purest form, should be poetry. For many people, it is the ultimate creative format. It's certainly true that anybody can prop a bucket over a door with a broomstick in order to soak some poor schmuck who deserves it, but is that what you *really* want marked down by your name in the history books? "He put a bucket of water over a door."

No, I think not.

The best revenge stunts are those that require brilliant insight on the giver's part. The stunt should generate a sense of awe in the receiver.

One of the best examples of creative revenge was formulated in days of old by Daniel Webster. If someone deserved retribution, Webster would deliver to the target the longest, dullest book he could find with a note stating, "Frankly, I think the references to you in this work are scandalous, and I don't understand why you haven't sued for libel."

See?

That elusive shred of creativity. Hard to think up, but easy to do and magnificently subtle in its execution.

A more modern example. We all know how junk mail, in direct opposition to Pasteur's conclusions, can spontaneously come to life like some sort of evil worm from outer space, taking on a life of its own and reproducing into infinity.

If you dare to send in a reply, ask a simple question, apply for a card, or even purchase a pair of rotary nose-hair removers, and you'll find your name has been sold to everyone from the U.S. Marines to a myriad of purveyors of pornographic materials and related items.

Any fool can take the postpaid envelope supplied with these catalogs of cacophony and send it back to the offending company with a simple, but polite, "No, thank you." But how creative is that?

I say, take that final, subtle step. Fill the envelope with rocks and write "special delivery" on the front. Now you've gone from a twenty-two-cent "No, thank you" to a sit-up-and-take-notice insult. The extra effort on your part will result in the outlay of many dollars on the part of the offender, only to learn that you're not interested in sex-organ extender creams.

Believe me, this will cause notice at the receiving end. You'll probably be taken off that mailing list, if not others as well.

If enough people were to do this . . .

I'm sure you get the idea.

HIGH-TECH PERSONAL REVENGE

ACOUSTIC CRAZINESS

A relatively virgin area of the revenge world is the use of acoustic ultrasonic energy to disorient and disrupt victims. In plain English, this means using sound that is above the frequencies of normal hearing to fuck with people. Ultrasonic sound normally starts at about 15,000 or 16,000 cycles and works its way upward.

Although devices capable of creating such sound levels have been available to the scientific world for years, the cost of the transducers (that is, the "speakers") has been high enough to keep these devices out of the hands of amateur social experimenters. However, the advent of the piezoelectric tweeter—a miniature, high-frequency transducer for use in higher-end stereo systems—has brought the use of such devices within the realm of serious pranksters.

Ultrasonic sound is, by definition, inaudible. However, every individual will have a varying response to these sounds. Because of this, the following units will produce significantly different results on different targets. It is safe to say that in almost all cases, some response will be noted.

The two units detailed here vary abruptly in price and in their pain-producing threshold. Both will work on people and animals. Dogs in particular can't stand these units. A number of successful experiments have been carried out by persons known to me to "train" a neighbor's barking dog to have a bit more understanding of the concept of privacy.

SINGLE-TRANSDUCER ULTRASONIC GENERATOR

The first device is a single-transducer ultrasonic generator capable of directional transmission of time-variant ultrasonic energy. The "noise" produced by this device will be at the upper limit or above most people's hearing (it has been my experience that people with very fine upper-hearing borders are able to notice the sound of the unit when asked to do so). The frequency is high enough, however, that most people would not realize any sound was present without a reason to listen for it.

In order to test the validity of this statement, it is only necessary to point this unit from a distance of five or ten feet at a crowd of people who have been prewarned and notice their reactions. In my experience, women tend to be bothered more than men, but almost everyone reacts in some manner to the unpleasant intrusion of ultrasonic energy.

How do people react? They will feel an unwanted sense of pressure and irritation, even though it is generally impossible to pinpoint the reason or direction of the unpleasant energy, as high frequency and ultrasonic sound waves tend to appear nondirectional to most humans.

Even though this device is small and can be constructed for a few dollars, the unpleasant

Packaged Irritation. For about $20, you can construct this ultrasonic confusion machine. Amazingly effective, it's guaranteed to irritate, piss off, or disable most of the human race from a distance. It's almost impossible to see, difficult to locate, and surprisingly effective.

reactions it will garner are nothing less than phenomenal. When exposed to the unit for any length of time, the victim will commonly become irritable. They may complain of a headache, little things will bother them, their eyes may water, and it may produce a feeling of vertigo or even extreme nausea in particularly sensitive people.

To reiterate, this small unit emits a high-pitched noise that is almost impossible to hear but which will invariably produce a feeling of unpleasantness and physical discomfort in the subject after some exposure.

The unit is powered by an internal nine-volt battery that gives it enough strength to last for several hours. It can also be turned on indefinitely by the addition of a nine-volt battery charger/power supply available from any electronic-supply store.

The unit is small enough to hide inside a hollowed-out book, radio, lamp, computer, or any other object that can be placed in the immediate vicinity of the target.

One particularly interesting application the author observed was when the unit was taped above a false ceiling (the kind found in many offices) and aimed down on the intended victim. After a short time, the person (in this case, a rather obnoxious employer) became more irritable than usual, broke pencils, snapped at people, and eventually went home early with what he described as a splitting headache, thus removing a source of unpleasant behavior without it causing any permanent damage.

The unit can be purchased on a set frequency (which happens to be one most dogs can't stand), making it a legitimate warding-off device for joggers, hikers, bicyclists, and others who wish to leave the .44 magnum in the drawer when they are exercising or who simply want to convince the neighbor's dog to stop barking.

The unit can also be purchased with a variable control on the generator that allows fine tuning in order to select the frequency that appears to be particularly offensive to any target.

This device can be employed in an intermittent fashion, bringing about what I call the "earthquake effect." The target will often look at his tormentors or other people in the vicinity and ask, "Did you feel that? What was that? Did you hear that? Wow!" or other exclamations of confused agony. The incomprehensibility of ultrasonic sound is one of its strongest advantages. There seems to be nothing there to complain about, but there is . . .

I personally recommend this unit. For the outlay of only a few bucks, it can provide the semiserious nasty person with a variety of pleasant experiments in the fine art of subtle revengemanship.

This device, as well as the following one, can be built from simple plans (not advised) or purchased for about fifty dollars in kit form or seventy-five dollars in a completed version from Information Unlimited (see the Suppliers chapter at the end of the book for address).

PAIN-FIELD GENERATOR

Imagine the effect if one were to take the ultrasonic generator one or possibly two steps further . . .

A number of government researchers have done just that, producing devices designed for riot control and crowd disruption. Think of them as sonic versions of CS tear gas. These devices are so effective that they are being considered by various state and government agencies for regulation and/or licensing, in much the same fashion as firearms. I am not implying that the BPF4 is in any way, shape, or manner capable of inflicting the same damage as a firearm. The unit is simply effective enough that the government thinks its use should be regulated.

The BPF4 can be purchased in various stages, ranging in price from fifteen dollars for the plans only to three-hundred dollars for a complete unit. Granted, this is a lot of money to spend on something that has little or no practical application for most people.

The key here is the term *most people*. How serious of a prankster are you? If the device might save a person's life—that is, someone you might otherwise be tempted to push off a balcony or shoot—I can only consider it a fair investment for the money. If you are bothered by a loud, barking dog nearby or a neighbor or spouse who invokes the same reaction as the obnoxious dog, and you have no wish to poison either, you might consider this far less permanent method of behavior modification.

The BPF4 is built inside a 7x7x6-inch enclosure and requires the application of VDC at three amps via rechargeable batteries or by the convenient presence of a twelve-volt video camcorder-type battery. The latter will provide approximately one hour of the most irritating operation imaginable. This device is powerful enough to be used for property protection. By

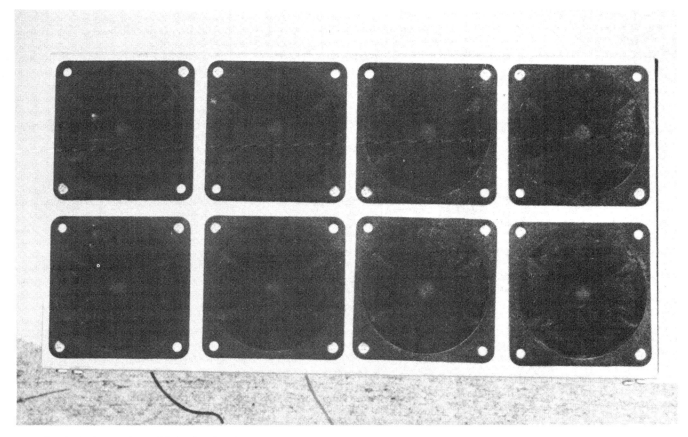

Revingist's boombox. **This device has approximately the same effect as a 100-watt ghetto blaster when it's going ballistic. The difference is that you can't hear this one. It will clear a path through the dregs of humanity or the animal kingdom, whichever is necessary.**

wiring it to a burglar alarm or other intruder-sensing device, the BPF4 can provide an immediate impetus to the unwanted trespasser.

The BPF4 produces a very high acoustic-pressure level composed of both sonic and ultrasonic energy waves and can be adjusted in frequency and sweep time by the use of external controls. The controls give the user an almost infinite number of choices, at least one of which is guaranteed to drive anyone crazy . . .

As the photo shows, this device consists of an array of piezoelectric tweeters (eight in this case) driven by a powerful ultrasonic generator. This system produces noise over a fairly wide frequency band. There is also a switch for an immediate 10x power increase, allowing the operator to adjust the unit for maximum output and most irritating sweep rate and then kick it into overdrive, so to speak, jamming the output into the ultrasonic range for immediate results.

The output of this unit is almost, as they say in the ads, indescribable. Imagine yourself lying in front of four-foot high stereo speakers with a sixty-watt per channel amp cranked up

9

well past the pain threshold, playing an album of someone sliding his fingernails down a blackboard.

Like the image? That's about as close as I can get to actually translating the effects of the BPF4 into print.

At one point during the testing of the BPF4, a friend of mine came in the front door just as I was about to apply the power to the unit.

I applied said power. She looked at me, turned around, ran out, and slammed the door behind her. To make a long story short, I ate dinner alone.

Granted this was not the original idea of the proper use of this unit, but it does serve to illustrate a point. As someone else suggested, this unit could be called the "adult's boombox."

A good image of this application comes to mind. Once I lugged my BPF4 to the local beach

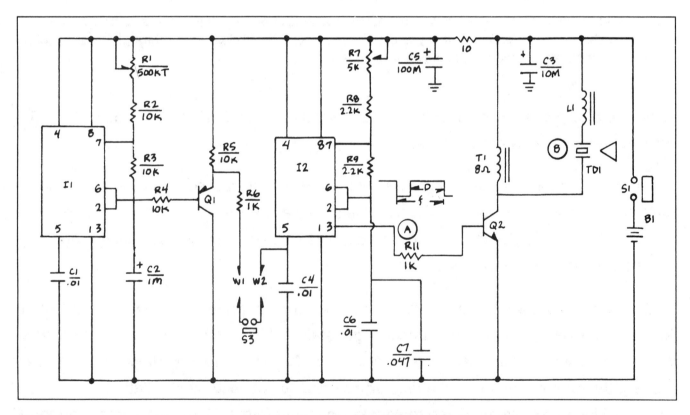

Circuit page for the pain-field generator. **R1: 500 K pot; R2, 3, 4, 5: 10K resistor; R6, 11: 1K resistor; R7: 10K pot; R8, 9: 2.2K resistor; R10: 10 ohm resistor; C1: 4.01 m capacitor; C2: 1 m capacitor; C3: 10 capacitor; C5: 100 m capacitor; C6: .01 m poly capacitor; C7: .047 50 v disc capacitor; Q1: PNP2907 transistor; Q2: D40D5 transistor; I1, I2: 555 DIP timer; S1: push-button switch; T1: 8 ohm transformer; L1: 1mh resonating coil; TD1: K1020 transducer; CL1: battery clip, box, battery, wire.**

on a warm, sunny day. Now, as with every beach in the civilized world, and one must assume even in Libya, our beaches tend to be jam-packed with normal, God-fearing, door-shutting, toilet-seat-putting-down, saying-"excuse me"-when-they-leave-the-table people. Yet there's always one dumb son-of-a-bitch who has convinced himself through heavy doses of illicit drugs that we all share his musical tastes. Unfortunately, these tastes always tend to run towards those rare copies of Whipping Madonna, The Rap Version.

This SOB invariably finds the best spot on the entire beach, which for some reason is always located within ten feet of where I've staked my property lines. Perhaps this goes back to my childhood when an alien gave me the strange power to attract the only assholes in a theater. This always includes two people who had already seen the movie and were dying to tell their friend every move right before it happened. Talk about killing Walt Disney . . .

But I digress. The BPF4 can easily be inserted into an acoustically transparent carrying case such as a beach, tennis, or gym bag, where it will attract little or no attention. This disguise is useful when some over-hormoned teenager who hasn't washed his hair in five days turns his boombox up to ten, as happened on this particular day. He was drinking tequila straight from the bottle, which he then casually tossed aside. He lasted about two minutes after I switched on the power.

The BPF4 is directional to a certain degree. However, you will notice there is some back splash, so you might want to wear earplugs or miniature headphones if you are going to use the device in close proximity.

If the unit is to be used for dog training, it is only necessary to employ the device immediately after the animal barks. After a short period of time, the little hairball will catch on and probably hesitate to even go outside, much less bark.

It is actually possible to hook up this device with a microphone so that it auto-reacts. When the dog barks, the device turns on for a few seconds and then turns itself off.

Although definitely an upper-end piece due to its price, the BPF4's possibilities are limited only by one's imagination. But for driving out errant roommates, creating schizophrenic behavior in the neighbor's vociferous, overtaxed dog, or putting a damper on obnoxiously loud beach parties, sports fans, or people who seem intent on making your life miserable for no earthly reason, it works.

While the use of ultrasonic generators could be considered an obnoxious move in itself, especially if employed by unscrupulous types to procure seats at concerts, stadiums, World Professional Wrestling, or other highbrow socialite events, it should be remembered that this device does not do any permanent damage and accomplishes one's immediate needs without digging out that black-belt-adorned karate gi that's been collecting dust in the closet all these years . . .

Not sold in any stores.

OPTIMUM OPTICS

The use of lasers for revenge or practical-joke purposes is a perfect example of cross application. Many interesting breakthroughs occur when technology from one field is applied to a totally different discipline.

In this case, we are using actual lasers, just like those used in surgery, seismic research, precision construction, intrusion detection, and the military.

When lasers were first developed, a ruby was required to produce the coherent light beam that is their trademark. Rubies were expensive, hence lasers were expensive and therefore only found in scientific laboratories or military workshops.

Today, lasers are much lower priced and relatively common. A modern helium-neon laser of one to two milliwatts in power, fully constructed with a high-voltage, rechargeable power supply and the laser tube (usually packaged in PVC tubing with a pistol-like grip), can be had for two-hundred dollars.

For those of you who have never seen an actual laser in operation, they do not resemble the science-fiction version. A laser projects a very small, very concentrated beam of pure light.

This light is of one color, normally red. The beam itself, unlike a Buck Rogers ray gun, is *not* visible. Only the glowing, pinpoint dot that appears on the target indicates that a laser is in use. Although laser beams do expand with distance like any light source, they expand far less than noncoherent light.

At a distance of four feet, a two-milliwatt hand-held laser will project a pinhead-size, brilliant dot of light. Brilliant is not the correct adjective here. The light is so pure and so piercing that it appears to be ethereal. It's not akin to looking at a red flashlight beam. It is a glowing, pulsating, intensely vibrant dot that simply appears on the target as if by magic.

A two-milliwatt laser will project this dot a distance of a couple kilometers, under ideal conditions (i.e., in the dark, not through a sheet of glass, and with the unit fully charged and functioning).

13

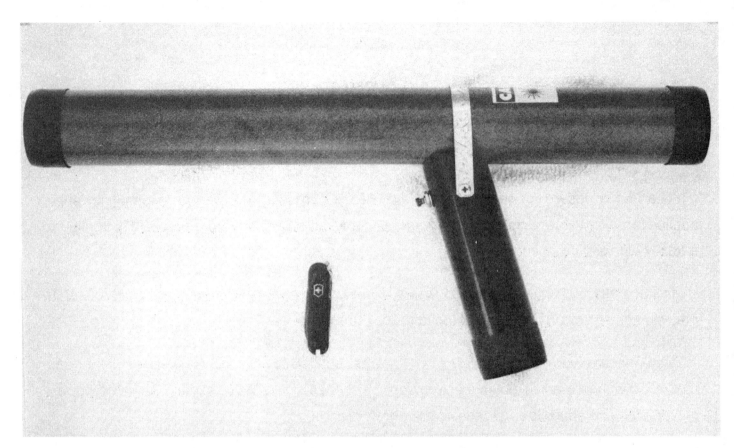

Laser. What can I say? This is a laser. This is fun. This can drive people crazy by creating UFOs, life forms from other planets, or religious experiences.

It is possible to bounce laser light off low-lying clouds or fog banks. By the time the light has reached its extreme range, it will have spread into a dot of an inch or two, rather than the pinhead size it was at the beginning. This is all fairly moot because the laser can be used for a number of fun and interesting get-even tricks.

BEFORE GOING ANY FURTHER, WE MUST WARN YOU: NEVER LOOK DIRECTLY INTO A LASER OR SHINE IT DIRECTLY INTO ANYONE'S EYES. THE BRIGHT LIGHT CAN CAUSE TEMPORARY BLINDNESS, AND HIGHER-POWER LASERS CAN ACTUALLY DAMAGE THE HUMAN EYE.

How do you use a laser for fun and games? The dot can be thrown several hundred yards, even in bright daylight, to appear majestically out of the ether on any hard surface. Joggers, ambling along serenely with their Walkman tuned to the local rock station, can be shocked to find a small, brilliant dot that seems almost to be alive, directly in front of them, paralleling their every move.

It's quite unnerving to be running along and suddenly see something—you're not quite sure

14

what—leading you on out of thin air.

I personally have seen joggers stumble, stop, and try to touch the mysterious item with their foot, look around to see if anyone else is seeing this God-like apparition, look up in the air to see if there is a UFO present, and even cover their eyes before jogging on so they don't have to deal with the mystery of the moving red animal.

Barking dogs are often fascinated by the laser dot. It appears to be a living creature of some kind, one they should chase and try to crush with their paws or bite, but the damn thing seems to remain just out of range. An accomplished laser operator can send a neighbor's dog running in circles, pawing at the fence, biting the air, or exhibiting other symptoms of mania that may require the dog to be brought inside or even sent to a psychological kennel for heavy evaluation, thereby removing his irritating presence.

At night, a laser could be shined through people's windows, even if the curtains are closed, to project a fascinating phenomenon on walls, ceilings, or even room occupants. This phenomenon rarely goes unnoticed and usually causes unexpected and often humorous reactions in people. It can be used to interfere with noisy parties or simply create mental instability in one's favorite set of obnoxious neighbors.

To this very end I've seen my own laser utilized (by a friend, not me) when some neighbors of an unknown ethnic persuasion were having a family get-together, a ceremonial sit-down dinner of some sort. Perhaps the dinner was in honor of their ancestors since a number of bronze idols were present, as well as burning incense, flags, and ceremonial dress.

In the middle of the dinner, possibly in the middle of a prayer, as everyone was quiet with hands folded and eyes firmly fixed on an elderly gentleman giving the benediction, a sudden blindingly red mark of Cain appeared on the elder gentleman's forehead. The reaction of the diners was both (a) instantaneous and (b) entertaining, as they leapt from their seats, bowed, and even rushed forward to caress the old man's forehead. This all occured within a two-second application of the laser beam.

The old man, who had seen nothing, began to enjoy his enhanced quasi-religious status. My friend could see from his vantage point that even the younger members of the family were not sure what had transpired and, despite their Western conditioning, were becoming quite enthused with what the old man had to say.

I would like to think that this was an instance of electronics making someone's life better and actually reinstilling basic family values to an otherwise mundane family get-together.

In another instance of effective laser application, a dear friend was having problems with teenagers using his small, residential street as an impromptu drag strip. Every evening without fail, a number of teenagers would gather, rev their engines, squeal their tires, and peel down the street at speeds of up to sixty miles per hour. Sometimes they would do this in tandem, taking up both lanes in order to see who would win the race.

My friend was the father of two small children who played outside, occasionally in the street. Pictures of road pizza films from his high school driver's education class constantly floated through his mind. To his credit, he tried almost every legal application known to man, including numerous calls to the police and county sheriff, but because he was in a rather rural location and these were low-priority calls, the law-enforcement agencies rarely found the time to respond.

One of his neighbors actually suggested that a couple of the kids he had recognized doing the drag racing were, in fact, children of the law-enforcement officers. Apparently, their street had been sanctioned as sort of a raceway for the Road Warriors. The street had simply been given to the young hordes in order to placate their adventurous tastes and keep them from the more populated areas downtown.

My friend thought of using caltrops or simply spreading Teflon-laced oil around curves, but he realized that either of these solutions would probably cause heavy damage and possibly bodily harm to the participants—a little bit farther than he wanted to go. On the other hand, he needed the offensive racing stopped. So what did he do?

One dark evening he positioned himself *behind* the drag-racing cars. As they left the line and squirmed off down the street, he flicked on his laser and positioned the dot so it hit the rearview mirrors of the speeding cars.

Effect? Immediate slamming on of brakes, sidewise skidding, and people jumping out of cars to search for the multitude of police cars that had the power to throw a blinding, multi-faceted red beam directly into their vision via the rearview mirror, or the aliens that had the necessary weapons to accomplish the same end.

It took about three cars before the kids decided that whatever the problem was, the solution was simple: move elsewhere.

They did.

One has to experience the effects of a laser beam bouncing off a mirror to realize just how effective this treatment can be. Although not permanently blinding, it certainly draws one's attention and reminds one of *War of the Worlds* or something more horrific, without any way to trace it back to the source.

In summation, a laser can be directed at a person, house, animal, or vehicle with astounding results. Only a person trained in the use of a laser would recognize exactly what that glowing, attention-getting dot of liquid color really is. To other people, it seems to evoke some sort of cellular memory of early humanic horror and will interrupt any activity it is directed at, if not cause the participants to decide they might be better off elsewhere.

And after all, isn't that the main goal of many "get even" techniques?

Besides, the damn thing is a lot of fun to play with . . .

TELEPHONES AND ANSWERING MACHINES

Because of man's reliance on telephone answering machines for his personal and business affairs, they offer a great deal of leverage when one's thinking turns to revenge.

If you have even momentary access to a target's answering machine, the most important thing you can do is to look at the brand and/or model. Most of today's answering machines utilize remote message pickup and remote outgoing message change. These facts are the mythical doorway that enable outsiders—with a grudge—to cause great mental anguish and psychological havoc.

Different machines have different levels of security, depending on their price and age. Earlier, cheaper machines use a one-tone code for both remote retrieval and message change. To attack this level of answering machine, it is simply necessary to dial up the number and during the "Hello, I'm not at home" announcement, press a button on a touch-tone phone.

If nothing happens, call back and repeat the procedure, except press a different number.

If it's an older answering device, one of the first ten calls will rewind the machine and play messages back to you. Another will probably erase all messages currently on the machine. A third will allow you to add whatever your creative juices dictate to the person's original outgoing message.

Some answering machines such as Radio Shack models use hand-held oscillators to produce a series of tones, accomplishing the same purposes as the single-tone machines. If you think a target has one of these models, it is a small feat to travel down to your friendly "capital R, capital S" store and purchase a compatible oscillator with which to produce the same results. This method has the added Rubik Cube factor—it will drive the target crazy since he won't be able to figure out who is listening to and changing his messages and how.

More modern and expensive machines use a three-tone sequence to activate their remote-command function. One has to be very patient (a thousand tries' worth) to break these, or one must observe the target calling his own phone and note the sequence of buttons used in order to emulate them at a later, more convenient date.

Of course, just the numerous call-ins required to try and break a three-tone code are effective in themselves. Who wants to get a thousand hang-ups on their telephone?

Simple modem programs will dial any number over and over until they hear an answering tone. This is a painless way to produce multiple call-ins on a victim's machine, voicemail, or answering service.

A more serious program can be used to produce tones that will crack the answering machine's code without your ever lifting a finger other than to punch the "enter" key on your computer.

A simpler, surefire system is to dial the subject's phone every so often and simply lay your headset by an operating radio receiver. Most machines have a three minute incoming-message time limit. Still, several messages of three minutes' worth of gibberish light the beginning of the golden path of confusion.

An amazing confusion machine can be devised by calling up a target's answering machine, recording his outgoing message, and then recalling his machine a number of times in a row and playing his own message back to him. Most targets will immediately assume the answering machine has lurched (at the minimum) or that God has decided to teach them a lesson (at the maximum). Even though physically simple, this is a mental puzzle that most people will not decipher quickly.

What do you want to put on a target's machine? Come on. If you can't figure that out, you really shouldn't be reading this book. Keep your day job and leave revenge to those of us who feel that third grade was indeed the best three years of our life.

TELEPHONES: GENERAL APPROACH

Besides automobiles, telephones probably offer the most sources of amusement for any dedicated revenge seeker. Although some of these ideas are not unique and some have been overused, they are still valid and work surprisingly well, based on the theory that the more complex the system, the easier it is to make it eat its own tail.

If one has access to a target's telephone, there are all sorts of numbers that can be dialed (especially if a long-distance code is built into the phone or is on one of the push-button memory retrievals, as is usually the case). This includes calling major corporations around the world to tell them what you think of their products, making threats (with a voice-changing device!) to state and federal government officials who don't vote the way you think they should, and calling anyone of a series of 1-900 phone numbers across the world, such as the infamous Dial-a-Joke numbers in England, Amsterdam, and Japan (no, we can't list them because there have been some legal problems with these in the past).

One of the more popular services in England is called Tele-fun. This is an endless joke-repetition service that won't hang up until you do.

By using a computer and a modem, you can access bulletin-board systems, many of which encourage members or casual drop-ins to leave data, including phone numbers, on their service. If one were to leave a "friend's" phone number with either an offering of free hacking information or free computer software or, conversely, one could be more honest and say this person is a real rip-off artist who deserves your respect and an occasional phone call, the person will find his phone ringing off the hook, 24 hours a day.

Most computer hackers and phone freaks have no sense of time whatsoever. They enjoy making calls, enjoy having their computers make calls for them, like to get information, like to bother people, and often don't pay for their phone calls, all of which results in a beautiful formula for harassing someone on a nonstop basis. Many of these numbers will stay good for weeks, months, and even years because bulletin boards are not regularly policed and people often download the information into their computers and use it at a dull moment.

I know you've heard this story, possibly even read it in other books, but I swear on a stack of Bibles three feet high and on my dead girlfriend's grave (she was killed by a train while retrieving her high school ring from my car, which was stalled on the tracks) that this actually happened to a friend of mine.

He was living with his girlfriend and had decided that the initial period of bliss had passed and they should go their separate ways. Being somewhat of a chicken, as are most men when faced with a similar situation, he decided the easiest way was for him to depart for the weekend and leave her a very nice (at least in tone) note, suggesting that she, the dog, and all her possessions should not be present when he returned on Sunday night, but by God, he did want to remain friends . . .

When he got back, everything was as he had suggested. The apartment was not trashed. She had even left his precious bottle of twelve-year-old Scotch in the refrigerator. In fact, he was halfway through his first drink when he noticed the phone was off the hook and a voice was giving the time in Japanese . . .

This sort of thing means you do have to have access to the target's phone. If you have, one of the cutest things you can do is activate call forwarding, assuming the phone has the feature, and forward his calls to a creative and long-distance number.

Now it's only fair to tell you that these feats can also be performed without access to the interior of the target's home. If a person is willing to risk the FELONY charges involved with criminal trespass and misuse of telephone company property, it's easy to access the target's telephone at the outside phone box located on his house, at the nearest telephone pole, or one of the multiple appearances of what is known as "B" boxes between his house and the phone company's central office. With a telephone or an easily purchased telephone handset, it is quite easy to simply plug into the target's contacts and make these calls just as if you were inside his house.

No, the phone company doesn't want to hear an excuse when it comes time to pay the bill or explain why all his calls were forwarded to Anchorage, Alaska, for the past twenty-three days.

By the same token, you can drive a person crazy and cause him to incur large repair bills on a telephone system. You have a choice here. You can disconnect the telephone by painting over the contacts of modular phone plugs or wires where they connect to telephone company lines with clear nail polish (this doesn't conduct electricity and is damn near impossible to find). Or you can go the other route and attach a twenty-nine-cent Radio Shack resistor (several hundred ohms will do) across his telephone contacts. This will keep his line open, disable the phone, and require an expensive service call from his friendly AT&T subsidiary company.

More sophisticated approaches to the same problem are to use a copper pen used for etching or repairing printed circuit boards to design your own circuits, or the most sophisticated method (as we say in the trade, MSM), the use of clear conducting paint. This paint can be purchased at better electronic supply houses or occasionally at auto convenience repair stores, where it is sold as part of a kit to repair the transparent antennas on windshields of many modern cars.

This transparent conductive paint is used as an electronic lead from the actual antenna wire to the interior of the vehicle so as not to interfere with the driver's vision. This amazing stuff is just about impossible to see and will conduct electricity, shorting out circuits as effectively as copper wire.

If lines are drawn between a subscriber's phone pairs, they will parallel the pairs, in effect making the phone a party line and confusing the hell out of everyone. If drawn across, they will short out the pairs. Very hard to find, very easy to do.

If you have momentary physical access to a telephone, amazing things can be done with super glue, such as gluing buttons up or down or gluing the hook switch so that it won't move. Few things in this world are as frustrating as trying to answer a telephone which refuses to let you.

"Hello . . . Hello . . . Hello . . ."

It's also possible to call the local telephone company and claim that you are the target in question. At this point a number of things can be done, from disconnecting the phone to a more creative approach of demanding a new telephone number because your ex-girlfriend is calling up and harassing you and you need your number unlisted. If you can accomplish this with the business office, they will not give out the number to anyone, including the target when he calls to ask why no one is calling him any more, which may take days or months. This kills his social life and drives him closer to that psychological red line in one smooth move.

The other side of this is to order call waiting, call forwarding, unlisted numbers, and any other expensive service your telephone company offers. Most targets won't notice the increase in their monthly bill for some time.

PAINT BY WIRE

In the last few years, paint guns (also known as "splat" guns) have become a continuing source of entertainment and recreation for people who have managed to avoid every major war but secretly wish they were out killing the neighborhood commie. Professional game groups create their own version of the Vietnam War by arming civilians with an attitude with a plastic "gun" that uses a CO_2 cartridge to project a .68-caliber gelatin ball filled with watercolor paint some distance.

When the ball strikes a target, it immediately squashes open, splashing the target—be it a person, inanimate object, or an animal—with brightly colored, completely soluble paint. Crouching around trees, park benches, or houses trying to "kill" one's friends with a relatively harmless but positive-marking weapon makes for a fun time.

A couple of factors about the paint gun make it extremely useful for revengists. The first thing most people don't realize is that, besides splashing you with a bright spot of fluorescent orange or green paint, it stings like hell if you're hit at close range. It can be extremely irritating. Right out of the box, this makes a paint gun the ideal choice for discouraging dogs, cats in heat, noisy kids, bad drivers, or houses that contain idiots.

The fact that the paint is entirely water soluble makes this a rather wussy sort of revenge trick since the paint, no matter how long it remains on the target, will wash off easily and completely with an application of warm water.

Of course, the target may not be cognizant of that fact, and a six-inch wide splash of bright paint on his brand new Turbo ZX Pro Dasher is enough to induce heart palpitations in all but the most steady customer.

The paintball combat games have gotten so sophisticated that it is now possible to buy paint guns that mimic the best modern weapons, including automatic pistols, rifles, and machine guns. There are even plans for sale that show you how to build a paint grenade.

The CO2 paintball gun. Like most things in life, it works better when you take the original idea and twist it just a little bit . . .

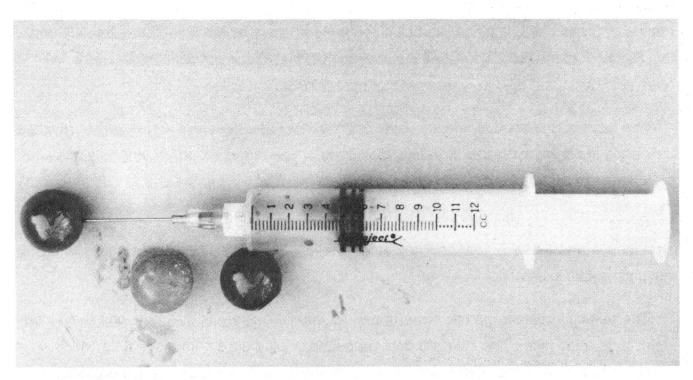

. . . and here's how to twist the paintball concept. A large-bore hypodermic needle can load and unload the gelatin balls as easy as one, two, three. And the leopard changed his spots.

26

The real key to the use of a paint gun as a revenge tool is the fact that, with a bit of patience, the marvelous little paintballs can be unloaded and reloaded. A large-gauge hypodermic needle can be inserted into the gelatin capsule and the material inside withdrawn and replaced with whatever you desire.

This trick has been done commercially and there are CS and CN tear gas stun balls already on the market. These are designed to be shot so they impact near a subject's face (note the disclaimer "near"), releasing a sizeable amount of irritating gas directly on the subject.

Simpler applications include replacing the water-soluble paint with insoluble paint, lacquer, enamel, or varnish. For interesting special effects, the balls can be filled with the contents from a chemical light stick. If this projectile is shot at an offending object or animal, the target will literally glow in the dark for several hours, creating a most unsettling impression.

All in all, the paintballs can be filled with almost anything that is liquid or viscous, providing a quiet, medium-range delivery system that can be purchased at your local sporting goods store.

If you consider yourself a serious revenge player, you won't be satisfied with a mere application from a paintball gun no matter what the ball is filled with. How big of a splat can one ball make? What is the time on-target involved for saturation splatting? Certainly this is a step in the right direction, but it's hardly the ultimate answer.

One would have to consider the application of a single paintball gun to a target's house, automobile, or body to be that of a World War I Fokker plane, where the bombs are dropped by the pilot throwing them from his open cockpit.

Effective? Scary? Of course, but hardly the same results one could reasonably expect utilizing a B-52 dropping its sticks in a rolling box pattern or even the use of today's laser-guided smart bombs.

So what is the cutting edge in paintball technology? An Air Power Sabot Cannon is an eight-pound device that looks vaguely like a LAWS or World War II bazooka. It is charged from any source of pressurized gas, including CO_2 cartridges, bicycle pumps, air compressors, portable air tanks, or whatever you have on hand. As long as it makes air or gas under pressure, it can be used to charge and fire the Sabot Cannon. The device is electrically fired from a solenoid, which dumps the pressure into the launch tube, giving consistent muzzle velocity on every shot.

Shot of what, you might ask? There's some flexibility here, from steel or lead ball ammo (which has been used to kill game up to and including *elks*), stabilized steel sabots, bean bags, water balloons, water balloons filled with tear gas, water balloons filled with paint, ropes, tear gas grenades, fireworks, dye markers, and *up to one hundred paintballs in one fell swoop*!

A true gadget for the seriously gadget-oriented, officially known as a "projectile and ancillary device launcher," this is the world's most powerful air-powered gun.

Its flexibility lends itself to those long nights around the fire discussing ways to get even. I mean, this damn thing will kill stuff, capture things, mark things, rescue things, scare things, intimidate things, suppress things, or sink things . . .

And it will do it politely . . .

The Sabot Cannon comes in several models, depending on the features desired, but all models have the ability to fire damn near anything damn near anywhere you want with little noise, no smoke, and no flash.

Flexibility and scarability combine here to let your imagination run wild.

Accurate enough to hit open windows with small payloads (again, balloons filled with things as well as fireworks come to mind), the Sabot Cannon should be thought of as the physical embodiment of the more sophisticated laser detailed earlier in this marvelous book.

Thank you for your attention.

TV JOKER

Suppose I told you that for an outlay of a few dollars (or $40 for those who are too lazy to shag parts and want to buy it in kit form), you would never have to buy a drink in a bar again for as long as you live.

Not only that, you could also dissuade those rude apartment neighbors who feel God has told them to put their TV against your connecting wall and turn it up as loud as it will go. In the extreme, you can get even with your little old mother for making you eat all those string beans when you were a child.

Imagine, if you will, from the far reaches of space, a small electronic unit that can be held in any convenient pocket and will literally scramble the on-screen picture of any television set within fifty or so feet.

Consisting of a pulsed FM-modulated oscillator, this device projects the most annoying breakup lines imaginable. We're not talking snow here, but major movie disruption across the screen of any television. The unit can be adjusted for turning on and off different channels completely surreptitiously. No one need know you are operating the little beggar.

Picture yourself walking into a bar where an NFL playoff game is being viewed by a large crowd of vociferous beer guzzlers. Suddenly the picture on the television set breaks into a fair approximation of scrambled sex shows on evening cable. Furthermore, try to picture the intense frustration when the bartender is unable to stop the interference and the patrons are screaming for the management's blood.

Suddenly you majestically leap from your bar stool and "fix" the television, restoring the picture to its full clarity with a simple flick of your educated wrist.

Think you'll have any problems finding people to buy your drinks so you don't leave?

Think the picture will magically mess up in inverse proportion to the level of drink remaining in your glass? Think anyone will ever figure out exactly what you're doing?

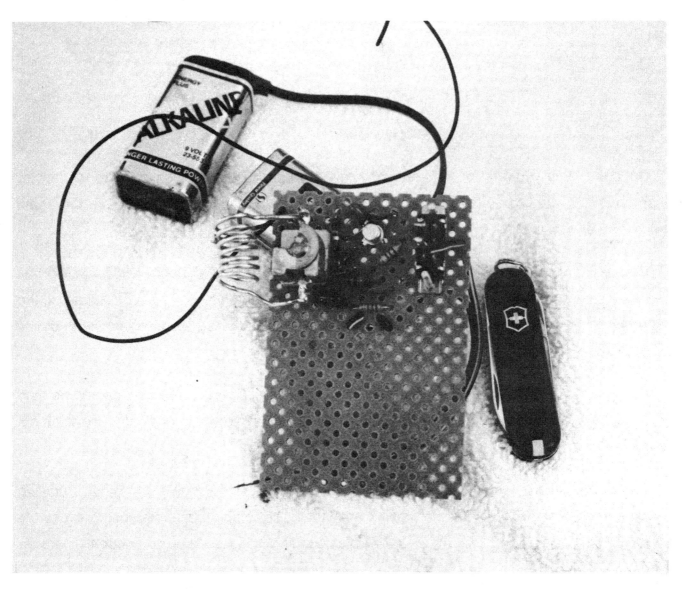

TV joker. **You'll never have to buy a drink for yourself again with the creative use of this wonderful gadget.**

Probably not . . .

This unit's signal carries through walls. It can also be used on boomboxes or other radios that are tuned to the FM band with much the same effect on the audio portion of the program as it did on the video.

While this device works well across a fair amount of free space, it feeds directly into the antenna of the receiver. If the television set is on cable, the range will be reduced dramatically. In fact, cable-connected televisions require almost physical contact for this unit to function correctly. Sets that are on any other type of antenna system can be driven, along with their owners, systematically insane.

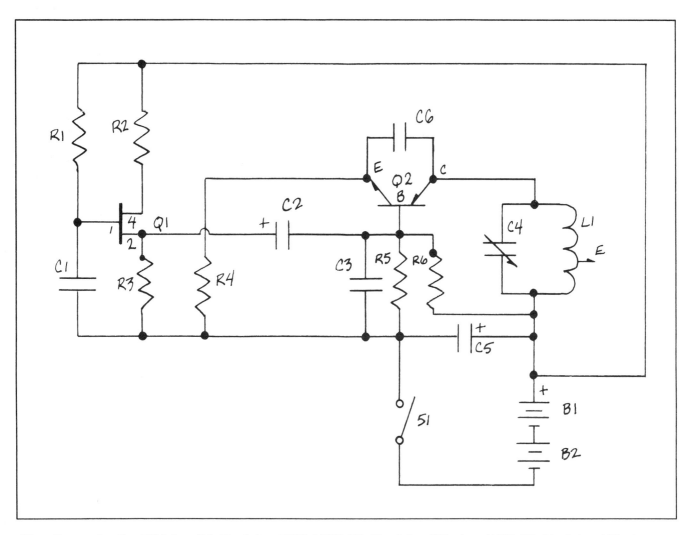

Circuit page for the TV joker. R1: Resistor 100K 1/4W; R2: Resistor 470 ohm 1/4W; R3: Resistor 100 ohm 1/4W; R4: Resistor 220 ohm 1/4W; R5: Resistor 3.9 1/4W; R6: Resistor 15K 1/4W; C1, 3: Cap .01 mfd/50V Disc capacitor; C2, 5: Sub2.2mfd10V tant, Cap. 1.5mfd@35 V tant; C4: Cap 2-20pfd mini variable; C6: Capo 5pfd zero temp; L1: 7 turn coil of #16 wire; 01: Semi-cond. UJT transistor; 02: Semi-cond. npn transistor; S1: Switch small mini slide DP DT; C4.2: Battery/holders 6" snap clips; 1: 9V ni-cad battery; B1: Battery 9V.

This device is pure dynamite and should be treated as such.

NO MORE COSBY RERUNS

Every book should have its ultimate fantasy. This section probably falls under that category, although the idea is valid and without a doubt someone will do it one of these days. Let me preclude this by summarizing the story of Captain Midnight, a gentleman who some time ago decided that network TV wasn't living up to his expectations. One evening he used a commercial uplink to beam his own signal to a network satellite, interrupting commercial programming worldwide with his own little tasteful message, "Hello from Captain Midnight."

They caught him without too much trouble. Why? Because old Captain Midnight used one of the few commercial uplinks in the country for his hijinks. There are only so many transmitters, so many dishes, so many places, and so many people with keys. You know the story from here. It's a Lawrence Sanders detective novel. Take one list, cross-reference it with another, and before long there's the perpetrator standing out in bas-relief.

If a person really wanted to drive a television network stone-ass crazy for some reason, or simply felt that their home videos were by far superior to normal game-show programming, and was willing to spend a few thousands bucks, it would be the proverbial piece of cake . . .

It's no problem to purchase satellite dishes and transmitters capable of beaming a signal to any satellite, if one so chooses. The important premise here is that satellites are not, or at least as of this writing, security conscious.

Birds, as satellites are known, simply take the strongest signal, amplify it, and rebroadcast it to downlinks all over the country. Satellites are not "smart." They have no built-in method for determining if a) the signals they are rebroadcasting are the legitimate signals produced by a television network, or b) where the signals came from.

Hypothetically speaking, let's say someone took their satellite dish and transmitter to a desert area in a sparsely populated western state, say Arizona or Utah, stashed it in an old shed or even a self-storage area somewhere, pointed the dish at a network satellite, and then electronically set the device to transmit for short intervals at *random periods* so no tracing sequence would be evoked. One could actually go on the air at almost any time one felt like it.

Satellites have no way of telling where the signal originates. If your signal is stronger than the "legitimate" signal, the bird will lock on your signal and rebroadcast it throughout the world. The only way to find the source of a signal like this would be to hire God knows how many airplanes with God knows how many receivers and God knows how many signal tracers and fly patterns over every state that might conceivably be involved for twenty-four hours a day, waiting for the dish to click on so they could try to triangulate the signals in order to locate the offending transmitter.

Do you have any idea how long this would take? How many executives would jump out third-story windows before the process was complete? How many viewers would actually start to look forward to your productions as opposed to those of Steven Spielberg or Ron Howard?

Extrapolate on this concept to the ultimate. A serious network hacker wouldn't place one dish in one state. He'd rent three or four self-storage transmitter points in three or four states and then randomly key them to drive people crazy and bring down civilization as we know it.

ON A SMALLER SCALE

How do you get even with or for that matter even force a radio or television station or network to pay attention to you, a critical member of the viewing audience?

Write them a letter? Well, I gotta be honest with you here. Although they like viewer loyalty, most stations expect a certain percentage of their audience to disagree with their programming or their announcers and figure these people will be transitory by nature. Their actions are known as "churning."

The basic school of thought is that just as these people become tired of a station's obnoxiousness, enough people will be tired of the competition's to even the situation out in the long run.

I once personally saw a vice president of a major network read a letter from a listener with a legitimate complaint about something one of their announcers had said that was flat-out untrue. The V.P. crunched the letter into a small ball, bounced it off the wall into a trash basket, and said, "Well, if he doesn't like it, that's tough. That's why they put buttons on radios. Let him take his business elsewhere."

I don't mean to imply that listeners or viewers are not important to the media, because they are. Unfortunately, a small minority of the population is far more important to program directors and executives than are the other 99.9 percent of their audience.

Why is this? And who makes up this small minority?

We all know ratings determine what shows are cancelled and what shows go into their fifteenth year of sitcom plots ad nauseam, but how many of us also realize that a very minor fluctuation in ratings can cost a radio or TV station untold amounts of dollars. Advertisers purchase advertising time based on ratings only—*nothing else*.

These ratings are not representative of the population at large nor are they verified in any major cross-section survey. Ratings are compiled from a very, very small amount of diary holders—people who are selected at random and are paid to keep a diary for a rating period in a specific market. In this diary they write down the call letters of each TV or radio station they listen to. The diaries are then mailed back to Arbitron (for radio) or Nielsen (for television).

From these few samplings the respective rating services produce what is known as "The Book." This book is produced in varying frequency depending on the market size, but averages once every six weeks for large markets.

The Book is the Bible. Advertisers, agencies, and media buyers all subscribe to The Book and follow the ratings as if they were brought down the mountain by Moses himself. These ratings are so important that announcers, program directors, and station managers live or die by The Book.

The rating services protect the identity of their target households with all the jealousy of a mother cat watching over her kittens. Due to the very limited number of diaries that are actually sent out, it is possible for as few as two subscribers to make a substantial difference in the ratings in a close market where a lot of stations are battling and only a tenth of a point or so can separate any one from the competition. This statistical anomaly gives each subscriber an inordinate amount of power.

Part of the deal the rating service offers its target households is that they are never allowed to tell anyone—not the neighbors, not the newspapers, and especially not the local broadcasting station—that they are a diary holder.

In the last few years, several radio stations have been caught offering between $500 and $1,000 to diary holders to list their call letters in their diaries . . .

So what does this all have to do with making some 27-year-old, snot-nosed, small-town radio exec listen to your important and necessary complaints?

You might consider writing them a letter. Yes, I know I said that wasn't very effective, but there is an exception.

Write them a nice letter (now remember, we are *always* polite), clearly stating your complaint in a nice, underhanded fashion. Suggest they do something about it or you'll take your listenership elsewhere.

Then the kicker—the final paragraph. "I know it's unprofessional not to sign a letter, and I would much prefer to give you my name and address, but I keep a diary and as such I'm not allowed to give out that information to your station. Thank you for your time and consideration. Sincerely, XXX."

This letter will send shivers of fright and visions of the unemployment line through any management personnel it reaches.

For television stations, target the editorial director or president of the station. Radio stations? You want to hit the general manager (who is usually a salesperson and knows full well what that rating diary means) or even the program director if you have a complaint about a specific announcer.

In this case, the pen really is mightier than the sword.

PAGER HASSLES

One of the marks of a successful businessman, drug dealer, or car thief is a small grey box clipped to his belt that allows him to keep in contact with all his important customers. This is accomplished through the use of a cellular network, where his office or anyone else with the right number can simply dial his paging service and summon him. Some of these services even offer an audio message on tape. The person gets the paging signal and a moment later a small speaker on the belt unit spits out the audio message.

Pagers have a potential for driving people bananas. The simplest thing is to dial up someone's pager and leave behind all sorts of creative numbers for him to call. Some of the better choices are those very expensive Dial-A-Porn or Dial-A-Stock-Tip phone numbers. The person is going to have to pay a small fortune for the call he makes back to the number. Unless he's paying close attention, he may not notice the 900 or 976 you-owe-me-a-lot-of-money prefix on the number. Rather than risk losing an important client or deal, he'll make the call.

Dedicated pager wearers can be summoned at odd hours, even late at night if they keep their pager turned on during times when they are normally spending a relaxing hour on recreation or sex. This can literally drive the victim nuts until he decides to change his pager's access number.

This is more of a hassle than it seems because the new number has to be given out to everyone who had the old number. Some people go so far as to put their numbers on their business card, making it extremely difficult to change their current access number.

If the pager owner is a bit more nefarious in his duties than the average businessman, creative number leaving can include the local police department, DEA hot line, sheriff's department, IRS audit section, or anyplace that would have a pointed meaning for your target.

Sometimes the simple fact of getting one of these numbers, calling it back, and hearing the phone answered, "Drug Enforcement Administration," is enough to completely change a person's life-style, often for the better.

To add insult to injury here, many paging services charge the person a set fee and then add a per-call fee if they receive more than a set limit of calls in any given month. This allows a target to not only get irritating pages but pay for them, too.

If your target has an audio pager, the range of implications is staggering. These devices are loud and obnoxious enough that not only is the person wearing the pager going to hear the message, but so is anyone within ten yards of the person.

If you know details his life-style, you can leave such messages as, "Call Lee at the State Department of Narcotics." I had a friend do exactly this to someone when that someone was in the middle of a rather large purchase of an implicitly illegal substance and with people he didn't know too well. The resulting chaos took much explanation on my friend's part, some threats on the other people's part, and generally created havoc. My friend has never forgiven the caller and to this day is still looking for the culprit.

Or he was . . . until he reads this story.

If the equipment is automatic, as most paging systems are, messages of a particularly explicit sexual nature can be left and broadcast to the victim during luncheons, dates, sales conferences, doctor appointments, or other situations of potential embarrassment.

On the other side of the coin, if you have a pager and are bothered by stupid SOBs who are too loaded to dial the correct phone number, here's all you need do . . .

Call the number that appears on your pager and inform the party that you work for XXX paging service and you're having computer problems. Ask them for the last number they paged because the computer ate it and it never went out to the intended receiver (who, of course, really didn't get it because you did).

Take this number and page the gentleman nonstop until he rants and raves to the real page company and gets a new device with a new number.

Never to bother you again.

ONE OF THE BEST

One of the best get-even schemes I have ever witnessed was put into effect by a gentleman who works as a private detective and bodyguard. He had a client who had been continually harassed (including physical abuse) by her ex-husband, who seemed to think court orders and legal suggestions were issued just to challenge his creative abilities.

Obviously, I do not suggest that you write letters threatening anyone's life, commit any type of fraud, or report false information. This is just a look at how a creative person can do a maximum amount of damage with a minimum of resources at hand.

The client didn't want anything bad to happen to the guy (although God knows why not) but still wanted the satisfaction of getting even. She wished her ex to grasp the fact that sometimes things can come at you out of the blue.

What the detective did was take a pad of paper on which he had drawn a rather crude map of city hall on the top sheet. He waited outside the target's workplace until he saw him coming out. Scratching his head, he approached the target.

"I'm sorry to bother you, sir. I'm from out of town and I'm supposed to meet somebody at this address. I think it's right next to city hall but I just can't find it. Could you help me get there, please?"

At this point the detective handed the pad over to the target, who examined the map carefully, moving it in several directions before he finally said, "Well, yes, your mistake is right here. Your friend who drew the map forgot to put in this particular street. You have to turn here and go over this way to get to the address."

He handed the map back to the detective, who grabbed it by the top cover, thanked the man profusely, and walked off. Our guy then withdrew a pair of gloves and carefully removed the last sheet of paper of the pad, one which he had not touched but which the other man had held with both hands.

He then went to the public library, rented a typewriter, and typed a note on the sheet of paper (which vividly bore the other man's fingerprints) specifically threatening to shoot the vice president of the United States on his upcoming visit to that city.

The letter was calm, purposeful, and obviously written by a man who had used weapons before and knew what he was talking about. He left enough clues so the Secret Service would know where to begin looking.

It didn't take them long. Those folks don't like threats of this nature, especially threats that can be backed up by the sender's fingerprints. The man was rousted at work and arrested. He had to make bail, get a lawyer, and suffer a fair bit of mental anguish before the charges were eventually dropped.

AUTOMOBILE MALICIOUSNESS

The automobile, besides being the second or often the first most expensive thing people own, offers a unique target for creative responses because it interacts with so many people in so many ways.

The revenge tips we're going to point out here range all the way from mild and harmless methods of letting someone know they really shouldn't take up two parking places or block your driveway to the severe comebacks which should be used with caution, discretion, and a bag of God-given common sense.

Let's start with a real easy one. Somebody's parked his lovely view-blocking van or RV not only on the corner but overlapping into your side street, making it almost impossible to merge out into traffic without causing a major accident. There are plenty of other parking spaces around, but these people seem to have what only can be described as the RV mentality of "Screw you, I'm big and do what I want."

One quick way of discouraging people like this is to remove the gas cap from their vehicle, leave it in a prominent place where it will be seen, such as on the hood of the car, pour a quantity of sugar onto the ground underneath the open gas hole—but not into the tank—and walk away.

You can make sure the person understands what's going on by actually leaving an empty sugar bag "caught" behind the tire or on a nearby rock. There are very few people who haven't heard the old World War II sugar-in-the-gas-tank-to-stop-the-Panzer stories. Whether sugar does actually screw up the vehicle or not is a moot point as far as we're concerned. We're simply banking on the believability factor of this formula.

What would you do if you discovered evidence that a pile of sugar had presumably been dumped in your gas tank? Do you drive the car to the mechanic and possibly screw up the carburetor? Or do you bring someone out to drain the gas tank completely and flush it with clean gas before starting the engine? Or do you just ignore it, assume it's a prank, and drive off with your neck muscles bunched tightly against the seat and your teeth clenched, waiting for that lovely sound of the engine coughing, missing, and stopping, never to restart?

This trick is nice because it encourages some rational thinking on the part of the vehicle owner.

A second or third warning technique after someone refuses to take the hint is to employ the use of caltrops. These devices look like a large version of a child's jack in that they are four-pointed, with one point always facing upward no matter how the device is thrown onto the

How to stop anything, anywhere. **These wonderful devices are copies of the ancient Japanese stop-the-samurai trick. Caltrops are designed so they will always land point up, whether they're carefully placed or strewn quickly. They can be conveniently positioned underneath a target's car so when he attempts to drive off, that's all he will do. Remember to leave a note. Always be polite.**

ground. They were used in ancient times to stop samurai warriors who wore straw sandals from following or chasing people, and are used today to provide portable, effective blocks for stopping terrorist vehicles by slicing the tires to ribbons when they are run over at any speed.

We do not advise ever placing these devices in a road for obvious reasons. When they are run over, the car's tires will deflate instantly and the vehicle will often lose control, causing damage not only to the car and occupant but also to the surrounding property.

If caltrops are placed under one or more tires while the vehicle is at rest, however, the tires will remain intact until the offending person backs up or drives over them, instantly blowing the tires and not allowing them to get up enough speed to create a hazard.

Very large and very effective caltrops are available from police and antiterrorist suppliers, including ShomerTec. It is also possible to make your own caltrop from a number of materials, from sharpened welding rods to pieces of lawn-mower blades welded or fitted together at right angles. See the photo.

All of these tricks are pretty useless without a note of explanation, perhaps mailed to the victim or clipped under the windshield wiper at a later date. How can you expect someone to modify his obnoxious behavior if he hasn't been informed of it?

Always give them the benefit of the doubt for the first one or two necessary behavior-modifying techniques.

Start little. Start low. A little mayonnaise under the door handle where someone has to put his hand to open the car will produce a shocked reaction (ever try to figure out what mayonnaise is when it's all over your hand and you're not expecting it?), but will cause no harm or damage whatsoever. If you feel the person is not bright enough to extrapolate his own scenarios, a quick note to the effect that the mayo could have been a variety of other substances will do the trick quite neatly.

AUTO DISABLERS

A more scientific method of controlled destruction in any four-cycle internal-combustion engine is to add styrene to the crank case. This chemical can be bought at body shops and upholstery repair stores as well as some shops that do fiberglassing, such as boat or boat body repair. If one were to add approximately a pint and a half of styrene to a vehicle's oil, you can guesstimate the engine will run approximately one-hundred miles before it dies forever.

This method is extremely hard to trace back and find the problem, as it will appear to be a natural "heart attack." It also gives very little warning time, which virtually eliminates the possibility of someone actually effecting some sort of damage control.

Throwing all attempt at subtlety out the window, of course, is the ball bearings down the spark plug hole routine. This stunt immediately panics the driver, yet it damages the valves and other crucial parts so quickly there is really no chance for preventative maneuvers.

Car batteries can be neutralized by adding a heavy base (alkaline) to their cells (even many so-called sealed-cell batteries actually do allow access to the cells. Simply pry the label

43

off and look). Where can you get a powerful alkaline? How about baking soda. Works well. Or for those of you who are more into prepackaged revenge, Alka Seltzer tablets will provide immediate relief to a battery that's suffering from excess stomach acid.

Attacking a car's exterior can include such mundane things as using some "quick strip" paint remover to write a lasting message in the car's finish, such as "don't speed on our street." To make this technique more subtle, replace the windshield washer fluid with paint remover. Besides being more subtle, this produces a rather more arty and interesting effect.

Brake fluid will also ruin paint, as anyone who's ever spilled a little on his fender while adding it to the cylinder can easily testify.

A more creative and far less damaging alternative is simply to go to your local auto-supply store and buy a locking gas cap for the make and model (they're pretty universal) of your target's car. Then simply replace his gas cap with a locking one. This is especially effective if the car is brand new and he hasn't realized it doesn't have a locking gas cap, so he wastes time calling dealers, trying to make keys work, or trying to remember if he borrowed someone else's car. At any rate, it's pretty frustrating to pull into a gas station when you're in a hurry to go someplace, get out, and discover that your memory has completely failed you, senility has set in, or somebody has put a locking cap on your gas tank.

To make the car run funny, a few mothballs in the gas tank work wonders. To put the fear of God in somebody with a new car, simply pour castor oil into the car's tailpipe. This produces a temporary but extremely heavy cloud of smoke that induces most people to think they have just burned up some valuable component in the heart of the engine.

Here's a nice one for targets who you know really want to stop smoking yet just don't seem to have that little bit of oomph necessary to take that first big step. Put a healthy layer of powdered magnesium in the bottom of the car ashtray (this will also work in a house). Magnesium is easy to come by, being about one step above a child's chemistry set. In a pinch you can also layer the ashtray with flash paper, which can be purchased from your local magician supply house.

It's these kinds of small, helpful tricks that you know the person will appreciate later, after he's calmed down and had a chance to think it over. Maybe while he's riding in the wrecker on the way to the body shop . . .

It's possible to shock and surprise someone with as little effort as loosening the screws that

44

hold his windshield wipers onto the car. Windshield wipers will stay in place with physical pressure until they are turned on, at which point they sorta rocket themselves from the vehicle. To add insult to injury, this usually happens during a rainstorm, making it difficult to drive around and buy replacements.

Another trick that usually goes unnoticed until it's too late is to dramatically change the color of your victim's headlights or taillights with red paint or windshield tint. This is a lot like putting a little sign on a car that says, "Policeman, stop me, stop me."

Although not entirely original (it's still one of my favorite scenes from the movie *American Graffiti*), I have actually seen people take chain, cable, or thin plastic rope, attach one end to a car's bumper and the other end to something stable, such as a fire hydrant, building, or bumper of another car. The cable should then be covered with leaves or other debris. This is a fairly extreme measure.

If you have access to the inside of the vehicle, a healthy shot of tear gas (especially CS gas, which is usually suspended powder) into the heating/air conditioning duct works wonders. It will remain there for some time and come to life when the vehicle is used and the duct gets warm. It's also possible to substitute nondamaging but smelly substances here, such as the various animal urine lures and ward-offs discussed in the next section.

A quickie that's funny and nondestructive is to glue a whistle to the underside of a vehicle where it can't readily be seen but remains in the air flow. This will create a most unusual sensation when the car is running, maddeningly ceasing when the car is sitting still and can be examined.

Another easy one is to collect or manufacture bumper stickers (there are a number of cheap kits available). You might want to say something embarrassing or, even better, very insulting to a social, economic, or racial group where the target parks his car. This really works. I had a friend who drove into San Francisco for about two days with a bumper sticker that made some comments about women that could be interpreted as unflattering. It took him all of two days to figure out why he was getting hate notes, lipstick, letters, and finally a broken side window and the inside of his car littered with death threats.

To be even more creative about this, place more than one bumper sticker directly on top of each other. This is in case someone decides the sticker is so offensive it should be removed.

They'll remove one, only to discover another underneath. This has the effect of sending the person into a deeper state of anger, after which he will do something more than just scraping off the bumper sticker.

The following trick not only works but is organic as well. Take half of a potato and cram it into the tailpipe. This will prevent most cars from starting, as the back pressure does not allow the engine to breathe. If the car does start, it will run rough and probably "explode" the potato out of the pipe with all the electricity of a nicely done fireworks demonstration.

In some states it's still possible to find commercial "car jokers." These little never-fail-to-get-a-laugh devices are constructed of gun powder, cardboard, and an electric ignitor. They are attached between the spark plug and the engine block. When the driver starts the vehicle, he will be horrified to see smoke pouring out from under the hood and then a loud whistling noise and sometimes a bang. Although this leaves no permanent damage, these devices have been known to induce high blood pressure and minor chest pains in the owners of expensive new cars or the wives of Mafia chieftains.

The rude version of this trick is to empty the shot out of a shotgun shell and ram the shell up someone's tailpipe into their muffler. The heat will cause the shell to "cook off" and take a good portion of the muffler with it.

Under the category of purely annoying, one can insert BBs, small rocks, or ball bearings in a hubcap and carefully replace it. The resulting noise is extremely difficult to find since it's only there when the car is moving and will send owners of new cars back to car dealers with stories of cheating and fraud on their lips.

The other end of the scale is a particularly disastrous tactic that a friend of mine actually used after he'd been turned in to the local police department by a neighbor for something he did not do, resulting in a couple hours of lockup and an arrest record (although he was found not guilty) and a quite noticeable social black mark as far as his other neighbors were concerned. It would have been possible to settle this episode civilly in the court named after that word, but it is very difficult to collect anything without proving intent to defame.

Instead, my friend bided his time and waited until his neighbor purchased a brand new car, of which he was undeniably proud. You'd think he had gone to Detroit and talked Chevrolet into letting him craft the damn Nova himself from scrap parts. Every two days it received a wash and wax job, and it was always parked carefully out of the range of birds, vandals, or killer trees, which are known to drip acid onto cars, causing unsightly blemishes.

My friend decided the idea was not to hurt the car or its owner but rather to reinforce his sense of social obligation to those around him. As such, he felt he should demonstrate how one species can live in harmony with another in close proximity.

He collected a number of beautiful leaves (it was autumn) and a tube of glue. In an hour, he transformed what could be considered a rather mundane and ubiquitous black Chevrolet Nova into a thing of natural beauty, covered with epoxyed-on maple leaves.

True, this event did take some time, but the result was worth it. It was not simply a statement of "now you're sorry"; it was art, pure and simple.

It also solved any and all further problems with the neighbor.

Somewhat along the same neural pathways, one can find kits advertised in car magazines that are used to etch the VIN (vehicle identification number) from your car onto the lower corner of a couple of your windows. This method is supposed to discourage car thieves because nobody wants to steal a car for resale only to find that the correct VIN number is literally etched all over the thing.

The chemicals used in this kit can be used with a nonnumerical stencil to etch subtle yet interesting phrases into a target's windows or windshield. Such positioning does not have to be done as carefully as with a VIN number. In fact one might want to avoid the less inconspicuous areas of the window and actually etch the phrases in places that would more prominently display the etcher's intent to both driver and observers.

Of a much more whimsical, albeit commercial nature, are those cute stick-on photos of a large wood screw available from gimmick stores in tourist areas. It's against my better judgment to plug devices designed by somebody else specifically for revenge, but I admit I love those screws.

When you find a car that has one of those unsightly, obnoxious, and inherently offensive bumper stickers with a large, red heart that read, "I ❤ my dog, I ❤ my cat, I ❤ basketball players," you simply take the screw and stick it over the heart . . .

Now the bumper sticker no longer says, "I love my stupid animal." It reads, "I screw my dog" or some other sociably unacceptable practice.

People who pull this stunt have at least done their part to remove one of the many unnecessary, uncreative, and, quite frankly, stupid eyesores on America's highways. Congratulations.

A black marker works well too . . .

Most motor vehicles can be disabled by a number of interesting or unique methods, particularly if one has access to the engine itself. For frustrating home mechanics, the quickest thing to do is simply swap two spark plug wires, either at the distributor cap or at the plugs themselves. Although this will not harm the engine, it makes it run extremely unevenly and while it can be fairly easily found by a competent mechanic, especially one with some sort of electronic testing facilities, it'll frustrate the hell out of the amateur mechanic trying to figure out why he can't get the car timed correctly.

The next step upward is an old favorite, yet surprisingly few people have ever heard of it. That's to take a soft graphite pencil such as those used in marking computer test results and draw a line from the cap of a spark plug or two or three down to the engine block. It can also be done at the distributor.

This action will cause current to flow down these lines, since they are a direct path to the block. Although the lines are thin, it still allows some current to go through the plug.

Again, this makes the car run extremely rough for no apparent reason. Even if the plugs are pulled and checked for wear or carbon, it is extremely unlikely that anyone but a reader of this book or an extremely competent mechanic would recognize what the pencil lines are and what they are doing there.

To take this a step further, use the "invisible" conducting paint that we mentioned earlier to seep high voltage off to the engine block at one or more places. The only way to take care of this problem is simply to replace all the plugs and wires and/or the distributor cap and hope for the best.

A large step up the ladder in meanness that should only be employed if the person had physically damaged your vehicle, nearly killed you with careless driving, or was related to you by marriage, would be to take plastic steel or quick-drying epoxy and carefully insert it into the keyholes of his locked car. You can imagine how difficult it is to unlock a lock that is now "one-piece" construction.

BRINGING THE WAR HOME

As almost everyone knows, the reason we not only have the space program but fight wars, killing thousands of people on both sides, is to increase the level of technology available to the consumer. You know: Teflon, better television signals, bullets that pierce bulletproof vests—all those things that are so necessary to our day-to-day life-style.

The technology of the Vietnam War is now on the surplus market. One of my favorite devices is known as the perimeter alarm. Perimeter alarms come in a variety of shapes and sizes. Anyone who managed to spend part of this vacation in wonderful Vietnam will certainly remember these devices.

Basically, perimeter alarms consist of 1) a bracket with which one nails or attaches the rest of the device to a fence, doorjamb, or tree; 2) some very thin but stable wire; 3) a spring-loaded firing pin; and 4) the alarm itself.

Small alarms generally use a small powder charge or even a .22 blank or a primer to activate their mechanisms. Large ones use .223 blanks or major powder-propelling charges.

What do you do with a perimeter alarm? You guard your perimeter, of course. Tired of people trespassing through your property? Tired of your neighbor slamming his gate every time he uses it, or worse yet, slamming his garage door at five in the morning when he goes to work, knowing it is going to wake you up and possibly drive you crazy?

One application of the perimeter alarm can cure many of these problems.

Simply install the alarm, run the wire where the offensive action occurs, and wait. These alarms are startling, to say the least. Even the small ones set off a huge "bang" and send a fireball twenty to a hundred feet in the air.

As we move up in size, we get the parachute models that not only bang and flame off but also gently float to earth a blinding, unearthly light composed of burning magnesium, usually used to light up an entire battlefield. The large units will provide several hundred feet in altitude and several hundred thousand candles of illumination. And they're not that expensive.

There is a legitimate use for these devices as burglar alarms or to guard one's property. They can be attached to items or across zones that need to be protected. But just the sheer joy of seeing the look on someone's face, especially at night, when he trips a wire that pulls out the spring-loaded hammer that sets off an explosive fireball directly in his path, provides the closest thing to ecstasy that most revenge seekers will ever acquire without causing someone permanent damage or accidentally ending the world.

Fireworks can sometimes be modified to produce these same effects, from simply throwing a string of them at an irksome dog every time he barks to setting up elaborate trip-flare arrangements. Yet they really do not lend themselves to the job at hand quite as well as the military devices, which were designed specifically for this purpose. Besides, fireworks are often more difficult to procure.

Military units are available from places such as Shomer-Tec, as well as a number of other military and hardware supply houses.

Another interesting device is the exploding target. If you are a shooter you've probably seen these. They are approximately the size of a bull's-eye on a regular target and contain some highly explosive, percussion-activated chemical, probably fulminate of mercury. When the target is struck by a bullet, it literally explodes with a clap that sounds like a half stick of dynamite.

Always a fun substitute wherever people are shooting, from range competitions to just plinking. They give an entirely unexpected thrill to the shooter who doesn't know they're there.

Exploding targets can also be rigged into emergency perimeter-awareness devices by the clever use of some string or wire, a heavy-duty rat trap, and the target. The trap is cocked and the exploding target set to be struck by the powerful spring jaw of the trap. The release mechanism of the trap is hooked to the string, which is strung across the zone in question or attached to the door in question. This is a basic "people's land mine."

When the string is dislodged, the trap and target will function in a split second, causing a stunning, disorienting explosion.

Lots of fun.

A great source of military and paramilitary supplies is Aztec International. They stock alarm signaling devices, booby traps, booby trap simulators, NATO trip flares, perimeter alarms, electric matches (allowing one to modify fireworks or other ignitibles to be set off by the closing of a switch), safety fuse, bird-control cartridges, and much more.

The latter are twelve-gauge shotgun shells that throw an explosive device about seventy meters out before it goes off with a flash and bang larger and more impressive than that produced by the good old M-80.

Understand, I'm talking back when an M-80 *was* an M-80.

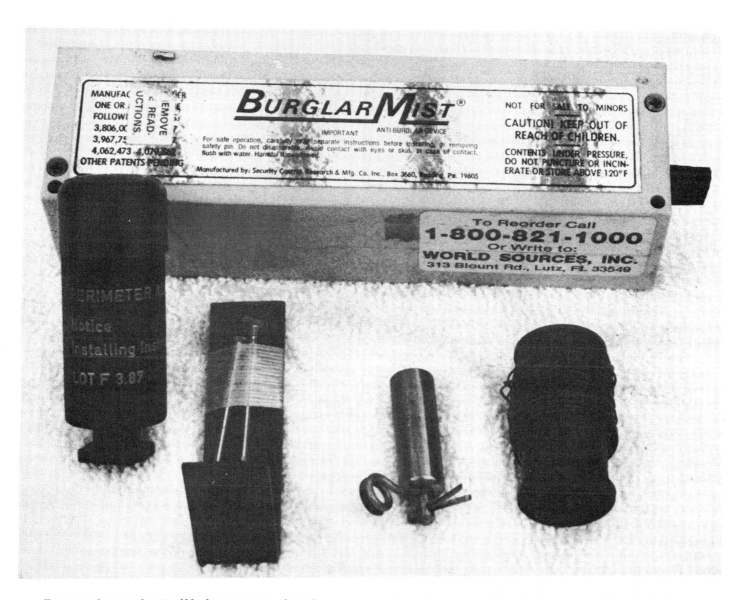

Protect that perimeter! Various types of perimeter protection. If you can't freak them out with a fireball, hit them with tear gas. Something's bound to work . . .

For a more penetrating but less shocking antipersonnel "alarm" system, one can employ one of the many burglar alarms that contain pressurized tear gas. These units are activated by use of a trip wire and as such can be hooked up in the same fashion as the perimeter alarms and military booby traps. While they're more effective indoors, they will work anywhere.

In desperate situations, where high levels of transgression have occurred, it is possible to hook both the pressurized tear gas and an explosive device to the same trip wire . . .

Flash, fun, and tear gas.

DOZENS AND DOZENS OF WAYS TO DRIVE ANYBODY CRAZY

THEFT-DETECTION DEVICES

Many libraries now employ theft-detection devices that trigger an electronic alarm when someone attempts to leave the premises with a book that has not been desensitized. The books normally have a small adhesive strip that contains the electronic code for the detectors to read. This strip can easily be removed from the book and placed upon the target or the possessions of some not-so-innocent bystander in the library. When he goes to leave, there will be an alarm and an embarrassing search and a more embarrassing head scratching and period of trying to figure out what the hell is going on . . .

Theft sensors in retail stores operate on a number of different principles, usually involving the "triggering" of a miniature, nonlinear transmitter by the microwave posts near the store's exit. While it is possible to duplicate this reaction, it's much easier to simply buy one of the tags from a clerk for five dollars, which can then be secreted in a target's pocket, purse, knapsack or even in a gift. It will provide an interesting few minutes of security mayhem, strip searching, and very probably an aggravated victim.

RESTAURANTS

Bad lunch? Waiters surly and unresponsive to your orders? Management's callous attitude embarrassing to your lunch guests, making you wonder why you chose that establishment to impress your out-of-town buyers?

Well, fear not. Many restaurants now do a promotion where they locate a large fish bowl, usually by the front door, in which they encourage people to drop their business cards. Every so often some honest, outstanding member of the restaurant management or staff draws one of the cards, calls the person up, and informs him that he just won a free lunch for two on the house. Not a bad idea, all in all.

In fact, it's such a good idea that I encourage you to improve on it . . .

Next time you go to the restaurant or even if you just happen to drop by to use the restroom, take a card out of your wallet, reach in the fishbowl, palm a handful of the cards already in the bowl, and remove them. Continue on your business as usual.

When you return to your office that afternoon, simply call the first ten or twenty people on the cards, informing them they have won a free lunch at their favorite restaurant. Hopefully they will even remember dropping their card in the bowl and will find your largess to be quite accommodating.

For a while your target restaurant will enjoy a cornucopia of good feelings from loyal customers who have been informed that they have won lunches. These feelings may migrate somewhat once the first hundred or so people show up demanding their free lunches, only to be told a small mistake has been made . . .

The only comeback from the restaurant's point of view is to honor all these free lunch requests. If by some slim chance they do that, you can capitalize further on their ineptitude by inviting not only yourself but all of your friends to drop by saying they received a phone call informing them they were to get a free lunch.

Then you might drop the manager a note telling him specifically what you found wrong with his establishment and that you hope now that he has had some exposure to other members of the community, he's had a chance to fine-tune his serving procedures and improve the overall manners of his staff.

POLICE KEEP OUT

The next time you walk past a site that has been cordoned off by the police, such as an accident scene, a home where a burglary is being investigated, or even just a construction area or barricaded part of a public park, you'll notice that plastic tape is usually stretched across the opening to keep the public out. This tape usually has some official sounding wording on it, such as "POLICE LINE. DO NOT CROSS," "DO NOT OPEN," "THIS AREA SEALED BY POLICE," "KEEP OUT UNDER THREAT OF LAW," or something similarly official sounding.

Simply tear off ten feet or so of this tape and keep it until you feel the urge to use it. If you want to really go all out, you could buy a roll of this stuff from a police supply house, but it seems easier just to drop by and borrow some from an unused site.

The tape can be applied in any number of creative fashions. You'll be surprised at how law-abiding the public will be when confronted with some official although completely bogus and physically flimsy notification of officialdom.

I once knew a man, as the story goes, who pasted the tape across his ex-girlfriend's apartment door. She came home and found the tape, freaked out, went to her friend's house, debated what to do for some length of time, called a number of people to see if anything gone wrong or if they'd been arrested, and finally called the police to find what they wanted her for and what the problem was.

It took them a few hours before they sent an officer out due to the low priority of her call, during which time she went through mental and physical changes and was denied access to her apartment simply because she refused to bend underneath plastic tape or, even better, reach up with her long red fingernail and split the tape into a thousand pieces.

USED CAR DEALERS

Had a cross discussion or misunderstanding with a car dealer? I know this seems improbable, given the high standards imposed upon this pillar of financial propriety, but occasionally it does happen.

A quick way to irritate and eventually cause almost any car dealer problems is to realize that car dealers, especially those of a larger nature, have an outstanding order to their telephone staff to accept all collect calls. This is in force because people may hear their ads on radio stations or see their promos on television stations carried by a cable network in another area and they want the chance of business that these calls could bring in.

If you happen to mention the incident to a number of your friends or, if one were mean enough, to leave the car dealer's phone number in a Reader's Digest condensed version of the story on a bunch of computer bulletin boards known to be frequented by people who like to do this sort of thing, it would be possible to inundate the car dealer with expensive collect calls from literally all corners of the earth. To add injury to insult, the phone operators and sales people will get rather irritated of hearing the story of your current misunderstanding with the dealer, not to mention the possibility of running up hundreds or even thousands of dollars in long distance charges.

MAIL-ORDER MADNESS

Many people don't realize that there are many products and services that don't make money for their owners. These operators make money, perfectly legally I might add, by selling mailing lists of people who would be loose enough to spend money on what may be an extremely silly product.

All kidding aside, the first example of this phenomena was the legendary rotary nose-hair clipper. It was sold at or near cost in small ads in newspapers, comic books, and magazines. The device was delivered and did approximately what they said it would, but the owners got rich by selling the mailing list of people who would spend five dollars on something like this to manufacturers in similar fields.

Each mailing list was sold over and over and over again. Figure a name on a mailing list costs about a nickel for a one-shot ad campaign, multiply that by several million, multiple that by the number of users of the list, and you begin to see where the profit comes in this form of mail-order merchandising.

Some fields are more known for this trait than others. For example, if you wanted someone's mailbox to be continually stuffed with irritating, insulting, and possibly obscene paperwork, you'd send in his name to a number of companies who advertise in magazines like *Penthouse* and *Hustler*.

Other sure winners are any sort of live-easy, make-money-now, mail order schemes, offbeat religious or social groups (the Rosicrucians come to mind here), or what could be the true source of the ultimate list, pick up a copy of the *National* (substitute your own word here) *Enquirer*, *Sun*, etc., and read the classifieds.

Look at all those out-of-work preachers and parapsychologists waiting for you to send your name, possibly along with a small donation, so they can contact you and try and sell you some sort of quasi-religious scam.

They then sell your name to hundreds if not thousands of other people trying to do the same thing. You can imagine how quickly these lists propagate, like a virus running loose in a mainframe. They replicate themselves and infect others within a matter of days.

More generic possibilities are time-share schemes, big-ticket sales items (always be sure to include the target's phone number here so the salesman will call), and anything else that seems offbeat or too good to be true.

Receiving all this unwanted mail is not only irritating, if your target lives with anyone else—spouse, family, parents, whatever—it becomes extremely difficult to explain all the plain brown envelopes with return addresses like John's Dildo Supplier that seem to cram the family mailbox day after day . . .

A variation is to send these things to the person's workplace, where the opinions of one's peers may be more important than in one's private life.

To carry the above suggestion one step further, make an effort to collect all those blow-in cards (the irritating little things that drop out of magazines while you're trying to read in the bathtub) and reply coupons that contain such key phrases as "no obligation," "you can stop any time," "simply return the books/records/sex items/Time-Life series on damn near anything from atomic energy to the Vietnam War."

Fill in your target's name and let him have the joy of spending part of his day writing nasty letters to companies explaining that a) he didn't order anything, b) he didn't want anything, and c) he refuses to pay for any of the items he's receiving so graciously.

This trick is especially good because he can't ignore it, as the companies will follow up with lovely threatening letters about destroying his credit and making him an outcast from not only his friends but the community of man if he doesn't pay them.

For your information, most of this is pure bullshit, but the letters are usually enough to scare anyone into prompt action, not to mention a number of sleepless nights.

If the above measures lie somewhere on the path you wish to take, but seem too passive in nature, consider going active. This is accomplished by placing an ad on behalf of your target. Most newspapers do not require any more than the cursory showing of I.D. (that is, cash) to pay for the ad before they will place almost anything in a public newspaper.

Think of something that would draw a lot of attention, such as an ad for a car at a ridiculously low price, followed by "This is not a misprint. It was my ex-wife's. I just want to be rid of it. The first $200 takes." Or offer to pay fifty dollars for some fairly common item that most people have in their home and want to get rid of. Place the ad to run over the weekend, since that ensures the widest coverage plus several days' running time before it can be cancelled. You can place one ad in one paper, a similar one in another, and a similar one in another. Before long your target will become extremely tired of listening to his phone ring.

POWER COMPANY

In about five seconds you can commit an act that has the distinction of duality. It will actually help your target for a while and then it will hurt him. This particular trick is even outside-approachable; that is, one doesn't have to have access to the inside of a person's abode in order to accomplish it.

What one does is take a large magnet and place it on top of the victim's electric power meter. You know, the device that has the little spinning disk in it and registers how much power an apartment, house, or business consumes in a month. Consequently, it also determines how much the occupant is going to be billed.

These meters are physically read once a month when a meter reader traipses out to step on your bushes and records the kilowatt hours consumed. A strong magnet will slow the spinning of the wheel by exerting magnetic force, which acts as a friction break so that there will be a noticeable cut in the target's electric bill.

See how nice we can be when we want to be? When the meter reader comes to read the meter and finds the magnet, he's going to know exactly what's going on. In most cities, his instructions are to report the target to the security branch of his particular energy company and sometimes to the police.

Power theft is a crime, and these ex-FBI-type security agents just love to get their teeth into a case where someone has, God forbid, tried to cheat the power company.

The results? There's a good chance he'll find himself prosecuted for power theft, or at least called in and harassed. He may even have his power shut off until the company decides to turn it back on. All this in just one or two simple steps.

You can improve upon the magnet on the meter approach by taking a minute or two to snip the little lead seal off the side of the box. This will sometimes go unnoticed for a month, then a new seal will be added automatically.

If it's clipped off again, the power company will assume that power theft is going on. To help this train of thought, place the above-mentioned magnet inside the box (with the seal snipped) on top of the spinning dial and your target will have one heck of a time talking himself out of the resulting charge.

To further increase his suspicious aura, back the dial up so it looks like there's a major dip in the power consumption for that month.

Gee, I wonder how that could have happened . . .

Although a very unsophisticated approach, this works well on technophobes—people who deep down inside feel all machines and the forces of nature, such as electricity, are out to get them.

ELECTRONIC GADGETS

Buy a little box of "blinker buttons" at your local hardware store. These buttons go underneath a lightbulb in its socket and cause the light to blink after it warms up. A target's first response to a blinking button is to change the lightbulb. This will have absolutely no effect, as very few people look into the socket to see if there's a foreign object in there. Most people don't even know what the bottom of a socket should look like.

If this is sequentially applied to various lamps, it will exasperate the target.

For about six dollars you can buy a little electronic device from mail-order suppliers that emits a high-pitched, hard-to-locate, irritating "chirp." You simply hide this device in the target's room or work environment and watch his frustrated attempts to find it.

I forgot to mention; the chirping stops when the light is turned on and resumes again only in darkness . . .

ANIMAL LURES

To offend someone's olfactory senses, a quick trip to the local hunting and fishing store will open you up to the world of animal lures. These lures are made from the musk or urine of the animal in question.

I don't know how to put this in a nice way. They smell like shit. Terrible stuff. If you live in an area that's populated with yuppies who wouldn't consider luring some poor animal to his death, you can often find the opposite—animal (usually deer) repellent.

This substance is made from the urine of obnoxious animals that deer don't like, and it too smells terrible. It's no wonder deer don't like them if they smell like that . . .

These items are effective when sprayed around a room, on a person's clothing, or in a car. For that especially pleasant occasion, spray some on a lightbulb so when it's turned on and heats up, the odor becomes intensified by the heat.

If you live in a very rural town, you can probably just get the stuff at Safeway. I believe the fox piss is located in the housewares aisle . . .

FUN WITH PHOTOCOPIES

To get a rise out of fellow employees, you can spike the office photocopy machine. In order to do this, take pieces of paper and type or write on them a) something that would bother the person very much if he read it on a machine in his office, like threats to his life; b) nasty rumors, or for that matter, nasty truths about the person, specifically naming him; or c) phony memos, including those that have the person about to be fired for some nefarious sex-and-drug-related pass at the boss's daughter.

Photocopy these statements on blank pieces of paper and distribute them throughout the machine's paper-feeding bin. This means when someone comes to make copies on the machine, it will copy their item but will also supply whatever you have put on the paper, as if by magic. People may think the machine has somehow kept an earlier picture stored in it or, in the case of threat-by-machine, technophobes will think the machine itself is threatening them directly.

It's important to distribute the papers, not just put them one after another so once after the second message appears, the target will go look through the next couple sheets in the machine and see nothing. Later on they will begin appearing again.

OTHER OFFICE MACHINES

Fax insulting items to someone higher up in the company than your target and sign your target's name. One thing you can consider here is to first take a copy of some obnoxious portion of your body (be careful when you sit on the machine, as sometimes the glass is fragile, and some of the earlier lights were bright enough to cause a slight rash) and then fax that under your target's name and return number.

Laser printers are a great boon for simple revenge stunts. With any computer and a laser printer, it's possible to make one-time copies of interesting letterhead. Both envelopes and a stationery letterhead can be made with minimum effort and without having to pay a printer to run off a number of copies.

Some of the typical letterheads that have been used in the past include the San Francisco

Foam thing. Did you miss the movie, *The Blob*? Fear not. Here's a complete Hollywood stunt package in two easy-to-handle, ready-to-mix cans. This wondrous material consists of two separate chemicals. When they are mixed together, the stuff begins to expand, overflowing its original container until it has displaced approximately 25 times its original volume! In about five minutes the queazy, climbing mess hardens to the consistency of plastic. Craft Foam will fill anything that needs filling, from a favorite vase, mailbox, or VCR to a small automobile. Fascinating, disgusting, efficient, and fun to watch, all at the same time.

V.D. Clinic, Ku Klux Klan, Herpes Foundation, McClellan Vasectomy Clinic, or just about anything else that would prove embarrassing to the recipient, especially if he has a spouse, family, or roommates, or if the mail is delivered to a place where others can see it (e.g., the company mail room).

My favorite story is of the gentleman who used to write letters from the Department of the Army recalling the recipient to active duty. The letters never included a phone number but always gave some military-like time (0600) to report to a bus station in a neighboring town for muster.

CRAFT CAST

Fill an offending neighbor's burglar alarm bell with Craft Cast expanding foam resin. You can be sure that you won't be bothered by those annoying false alarms again. Craft Cast has numerous other uses, such as eliminating all the unnecessary space in mailboxes, potters, plants, and even cars.

FIRECRACKERS

One teenager who I interviewed told me his best moments came from waiting until a target was observed sitting in a room in his house, especially at night. My "friend" would then quietly tape a firecracker onto a window facing the room the victim was in. At the appropriate moment, he'd light the fuse and then knock loudly on the glass, stepping back in the darkness to observe the reaction.

As best as he could remember, people tended to run towards the firecracker, run back into the room, run towards the firecracker, and some of them even made it back into the room one last time before detonation.

In all fairness, I should point out the gentleman I was interviewing was serving time in a detention center as he revealed this story . . .

SIGNAL HORNS

A great gadget for revenge is a compressed-air signaling horn available at marine supply houses. These small units come in a couple different sizes and produce an ungodly, horrendous noise when the nozzle is depressed.

This wall of sound can be used to startle people out of their shoes (imagine a diesel truck silently creeping up within two feet of your left eardrum and the driver yanking on his horn cord), blasted through walls to remind boombox and loud car owners that other people have to sleep, used to scare the hell out of dogs, or even employed as a substitute for the wondrous TV joker in a bar situation.

The latter use is best presented using a shill. Your shill sits near you on a bar stool without acknowledging your presence and proceeds to tell people he has just won an international award for being the world's best impersonator of that dying species, the whooping crane.

In any normal bar, this will be greeted with suspicion and rude noises. The shill offers to demonstrate. He opens his mouth for a brief period while you hit the horn, which is secreted in a coat pocket. The noise is so devastating and so nondirectional that, with a little practice, if you time it right, it will convince most bystanders, especially those who have had at least one drink, that some malformation in your buddy's windpipe has allowed him to produce sounds that would baffle Beverly Sills.

Although this really isn't a true revenge tactic, I'll guarantee that you can get free drinks for several more demonstrations.

AMMONIA

One of the simplest yet effective barking-dog stoppers is household ammonia. Dogs have a well developed sense of smell, so they react very strongly to the presence of ammonia. They hate it.

For under ten dollars you can buy a long-distance, electrically operated "automatic" squirt gun that will hold about half a bottle of household ammonia or its stronger cousin, ammonium hydroxide. As far as our canine friends are concerned, this is a quick, quiet, modification-behavior device.

VOICE CHANGER

Rude, annoying, and anonymous phone calls are beneath the dignity of anyone who reads this books. Right?

Sort of. With a little creativity, you can transform your voice into that of a total stranger, throwing in a sex change for good measure. There's at least one voice changer on the market that actually works.

The DVC 1000 Digital Voice Changer does a fair job of varying a person's voice from a deep bass to a rather nifty-sounding female soprano. The device only works over the telephone. You cup the automatic speaker over the mouthpiece and speak into the device's microphone. The DVC will disguise anyone's voice and with a little luck convince a target that he's being plagued by a horde of different anonymous voices.

For some reason, the device also has a barking-dog sound effect. When you hit the red button it goes, "Woof, woof, woof." I like this. I don't know why it's there, and the dog starts sounding extremely flat after a few repetitions, but it's a nice touch . . .

VENDING VENGEANCE

If you have access to a vending machine that dispenses its products in individual plastic compartments on a carousel or with individual slots, you have a choice. You can either super glue the doors shut, driving potential customers as well as the refiller crazy, or you can put in your $1.25, remove the tuna fish sandwich, and replace it with a plastic rat, a popular gag available at most joke shops.

ADDRESS CHANGE

Most post offices will accept a change of address request with a minimum of I.D. This will forward all the target's mail to a location of your choice. You might consider, Guam, Cuba, Africa, or a mail drop in Colombia . . .

C.O.D.

While a number of revenge books have suggested ordering C.O.D. items from companies to irritate a particular person, one must realize that this doesn't do much because the recipient can refuse the item. It costs him nothing and actually requires a minimal hassle.

On the other hand, companies that send sleazy materials C.O.D. are responsible for a set amount to the post office, whether the item is accepted or not. This fact can be posted on computer bulletin boards, shared with one's friends, or just creatively thrown into action in order to get a particular point across to a mail-order house.

There actually are a number of people out there who like to get junk mail. To put yourself or anyone else you feel like exposing to this wonderful world on a multitude of national lists, send one dollar plus your address and a signed statement saying you're over twenty one and wish to receive mail to:

Direct Mail Marketing Association
6 East 43rd Street
New York, NY 10017

INTERIOR DECORATING

If a revengist has access to the interior of a person's house, apartment, or business, there is a long list of quick one-shots that may seem simple individually but when taken together can lead a victim to the brink of yuppie insanity.

Divide the environment into horizontal zones. Consider items from the floor to three feet high, from three to six feet, and then from six feet to the ceiling. Start at one end of the room and work your way up or down.

Is there an aquarium? If it's salt water, toss a copper penny in. If it's fresh water, add some salt. If you're not sure what kind of water it is, turn the heater up to maximum.

Stereos and other electronic equipment have vents cut in the top to alleviate heat. Push a couple of straightened paper clips into the vents or, if you have time, force strands of steel wool through them and onto the circuit board. When the device is energized, the resulting light show will rival that of when the mother ship hovered overhead in *Close Encounters of the Third Kind*.

Stereo phonograph? Bend the needle so it not only doesn't work correctly but will damage any LPs played upon it. Any sort of tape player? Use the super glue-mounted magnet trick. Any tapes lying around can be quickly scrambled with a hand-held magnet. Computer disks? Scramble with magnets or mechanically disable with a couple drops of Karo syrup, super glue, or sand.

Fireplace? Mix black powder (purchased at gun shops or homemade) in with the ashes. Hide fireworks in with the ashes or wood. Do the same with ovens or grills. Pieces of aluminum foil can be hidden in microwave ovens to produce much the same result.

Use telephone tricks to make long distance calls, or forward the phone to some ungodly location.

Reset alarms, remove portions of books, steal small but essential parts like typewriter balls. Be creative and use your imagination.

DRUNKEN GUEST

If a guest is rude enough to pass out from drinking or misuse of some other social convenience, the incident should be emphasized in order to remain vivid in his memory. One method of doing this is to get the person into a bed and then use a couple boxes of Saran Wrap to wrap the person and the bed into one solid unit.

The startling effect of invisible plastic on a waking drunk must be seen to be thoroughly appreciated. And for God's sake, don't smother the guy . . .

SUBSTANCE-BASED REVENGE

EXPLOSIVES FOR FUN AND PROFIT

Although explosives are extremely unstable by nature and should only be handled by experts and really should not be employed for purposes of neighborly revenge, there are a couple of exceptions to this rule. One is hydrogen tri-iodide.

Before we go into this, I want to mention two things. One is a warning: do not make this substance unless you know what you are doing and can follow safety rules. *This is given for informational purposes only*!

Even a small pencil-lead-sized amount of hydrogen tri-iodide will explode with the force of an M-80 firecracker and is capable of tearing off a finger or two. Even smaller amounts can explode and will do damage relative to the size of the charge.

Now for the introductory story. I knew someone (thank God I had all these friends, huh?) who, while in college, was asked by the senior class president to devote his time and effort to make a rather involved audio tape for a play the senior class was to put on. My friend devoted approximately one week of his time to securing the music and using the audio lab to cut it up and generally get it ready for use. He did this gratis. After all, he was going to be a senior himself someday . . .

When he had finished the tape and given it to the class president, he was informed, "Oh, gosh, we changed our minds sometime ago and are not going to do that anymore. Didn't anyone tell you?"

My friend went home, thought it over, went to the chemistry lab, and prepared hydrogen tri-iodide.

About an hour before the senior class was to put on their new and revised play, he spread the mixture evenly over the stage, allowing it to dry naturally.

The play was a bigger hit than anyone could have foreseen. Midway through the first act, when the actors stepped on the scattered bits of now-dry hydrogen tri-iodide, it exploded.

For some reason, this drove the participants crazy. The show must go on, but actresses were screaming through their tears, afraid to move from one spot to another. Actors forgot their lines. The audience, although not exactly sure of what was going on, became hysterical with laughter.

Halfway through the second act, a chemistry professor took pity on the performers, stopped the play, and mopped the stage down with water, thereby diluting and disposing of the chemical. All in all, it was one of the high points of my friend's college career as well as many of the seniors who considered themselves budding actresses and actors, who today are selling life insurance.

Here is the formula for hydrogen tri-iodide, the world's most sensitive explosive.

This highly unstable compound has long been a favorite of college chemistry students because it is extremely easy to make and use. Hydrogen tri-iodide is, without a doubt, the most sensitive yet practical explosive compound available.

It is made from two common materials. The materials are so common they can be purchased at many drugstores, although most chemists and druggists are hip to this process and would cast extreme suspicion on any purchase that consisted entirely of these materials.

The materials used are iodine and ammonia. The key to the reaction is the purity of the ingredients. The iodine must be pure iodine in crystal form and the ammonia must be at least 20 percent strength.

It is possible to find 20+ percent ammonia available for industrial cleaning and laboratory glassware cleaning. It is also possible to buy reagent-grade ammonium hydroxide in even greater strengths.

Ammonia in this strength is extremely dangerous, and the fumes can not only be painful but harmful to living tissue. *Never* attempt to smell any potentially strong chemicals such as ammonia. If you are trying to use odors to identify the chemical, *always* "grab" a small portion of air and vapors and then smell the diluted version still captured in your hand. *Always* work with ammonia in an extremely well-ventilated area, using protection for your skin and a breathing apparatus.

Hydrogen tri-iodide is made by dissolving the iodine crystals in the ammonia until a supersaturated solution is reached. At this point, the mixture is filtered through commercial filter paper. The resulting compound—a small quantity of dark crystals that looks like black sand—is then immediately immersed in cold water while still in the filter paper.

The amount of product is extremely slight when compared with the amount of iodine crystals used. A couple of tablespoons worth of iodine crystals will produce half a fingernail-sized amount of hydrogen tri-iodide. Don't let the small amount of this compound mislead you. It is extremely powerful. As I mentioned, an amount equal in size to a normal pencil lead will explode with approximately the force of an M-80.

Once the hydrogen tri-iodide is prepared, *it is extremely important to be careful.* Any mistake could be harmful or even fatal to the handler. Two basic rules to follow:

1. *Never* store more than a minute quantity in one place.

2. *Never* allow the chemical to dry out. This compound must be stored in water at all times, preferably in a sealed bottle and preferably in a refrigerator. The chemical is so unstable that when it is dried out and placed on any surface, the touch of a feather, literally, will cause it to explode violently.

As long as this compound is stored in water it remains relatively stable. Because of this quality, it can be carefully "painted" onto a number of surfaces or applied to a number of common items. Once in place, the material will dry out, and the next contact with it will be an explosive one.

Historical applications for this include such surprisers as painting it in keyholes, on light switches, in doorways, in the inside of lip of drawers, and anywhere else that is exposed to sudden contact.

Adding a minute amount to the edge of a floppy disk or inside a disk drive would cause the disk to explode when inserted into the drive.

Talk about your computer crashes . . .

Dust-sized particles, too small to be seen with the naked eye, will explode with an audible crack when dry. If possible, the material should be stored in a vessel with a nonscrew cap, as small pieces may lodge in the threads, dry out, and cause minor explosions when the cap is turned to access the wet material

If one suspects one has become the victim of an application of this compound, the antidote is simple: apply water to any surfaces that may have been coated to dilute the material, then dispose of the water (which will contain pieces of the explosive) by washing it down the drain or flushing it down the ol' toilet.

OLFACTORY ATTACK

Only in America can one walk to the local discount weapons store or simply place an order with a reputable firm and have an agency of the federal government deliver amazingly objectionable and potentially dangerous chemicals to one's house.

Packed for use.

TEAR GAS

Law enforcement agencies have traditionally used two types of tear gas, designated CS and CN. CS is military tear gas and the less lethal of the two formulas. It actually consists of minute solid particles of irritant suspended in compressed air or some other compressed gas. CS is normally obtainable in a one- to two-percent solution. In this strength, one shot to the face of anyone bent on mayhem or a similar offense tends to effectively incapacitate the recipient by producing an immediate burning reaction in the eyes, resulting in streams of tears, temporary blindness, coughing, breathing difficulty, tightness of the chest, and a general feeling of panic.

This irritant can be applied in a number of ways, from spraying via a tear gas "pen" or small, hand-held cannister to the quick dispersion of a tear gas grenade all the way to fogging machines designed for massive crowd control that project jets of CS gas out to forty-five feet.

The effects of CS gas last for approximately thirty minutes. Then the chemicals evaporate, leaving no residue. Although extremely uncomfortable to the target, CS gas produces no permanent ill effects whatsoever.

Police and military agencies often employ tear gas in grenade form, which produces either a burst or a continuous discharge of CS smoke for ten to twenty seconds. Such grenades were generally kept out of the hands of the general public.

Until now . . .

CS tear gas is now available in an aerosol-type dispenser that operates much like an insecticide fogger. The can is set to discharge by pressing a lever-type cap into a locked position. It will then discharge its CS smoke for approximately twenty-eight seconds. One canister is effective enough to clear, oh, well, let's say a large indoor or outdoor party of bottle-throwing alcoholics . . .

Meanwhile, back on the ranch, the more conventional canister/pen units can be used in tight situations to quickly make them untight.

Because it is a particle gas, CS irritant will fall upon and stick to surfaces, where it will remain for some time and be kicked up or disturbed by people walking through it or sitting on it (as in a car). It will cause some irritation in this fashion, although not as much as when it's dispersed by spraying or grenade release.

PEPPER GAS

A few years ago, an unknown gentleman was peeling red peppers for his version of chicken Mexicana when he accidentally rubbed his eyes with the oil impregnated on his fingertips. The rest, as they say, is history . . .

Sold under a variety of brand names, including Cap-Stun, this invisible, nonlethal gas is a totally organic product derived from red peppers, or to be technically correct, oleoresin capsicum. It is used exactly like conventional tear gas aerosols and comes packaged similar to tear gas in small, direct-spray pens and canisters, as well in riot-control grenades. It is publicly available in fogger canisters that can be employed against people rather than insects.

When sprayed directly on an attacker, pepper gas affects the mucus membranes and immediately causes coughing, choking, nausea, and temporary blindness. The blindness will wear off in two to five minutes, and the other symptoms will gradually disappear in the next half hour. Unlike tear gas, this substance is literally a gas and when a small amount is sprayed in a closed area, it immediately saturates all available space.

A good test is to take a small canister of pepper gas and apply a one-second burst to a wall. Walk to the other side of the room and wait. Within a few seconds or a minute at the most, you will begin to experience tightness of breath, choking, respiratory distress, and nausea, although there will be no visible element or odor to disclose the presence of the gas.

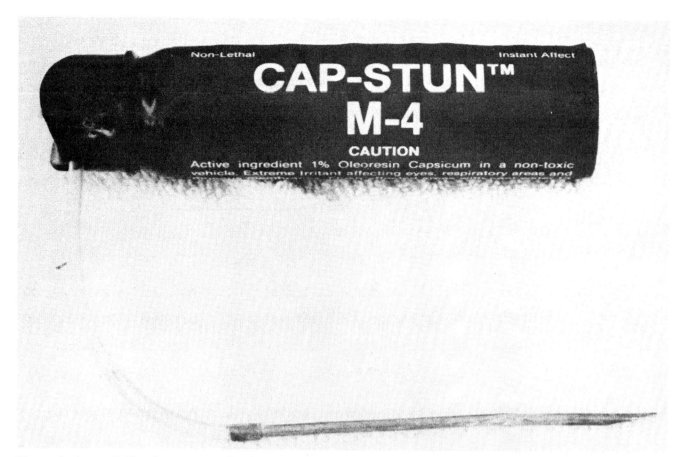

Through the wall. **Here's a pressurized version of Cap-Stun with a steel needle and plastic application tube. Under doors, through keyholes, or simply punched through plasterboard walls, this devices gives you a quick, quiet, invisible way to control dogs, dupes, dopes, duds, or drunks.**

Such rapid dispersion allows pepper gas to be used in situations where tear gas would prove to be ineffective.

If a small burst of this gas is sprayed on the floor near a victim's foot—say in a movie theater where some drunk next to you is spilling his coke on your lap—and then you were to walk to the other side of the theater, one would notice the drunk experiencing flu-like symptoms in a few seconds that would very likely cause him to leave the area or at least shut up.

If a small burst is sprayed into a closed vehicle or room, it will remain in the air for approximately fifteen minutes and still be effective when someone walks into the space. This option allows the revengist to set up an aerial booby trap if he knows where the target will soon be.

Most of these canisters come with some sort of directional nozzle to which a small plastic tube can be attached, thus directing the irritant under a door or in the cracks of a window to attack specific target areas.

Along the same lines, a four-dollar device known as an auto-ejector is available from Shomer-Tec. The auto-ejector fits over the nozzle of Cap-Stun dispenser units and passes the pepper gas through a plastic tube into a 4 1/2-inch stainless-steel hollow needle. This needle can easily be poked through the rubber gasket that surrounds automobile windows.

This unit was originally designed to allow highway patrolmen and other cops to induce someone to leave his parked vehicle without breaking a window or otherwise causing injury to the occupant.

It still works.

The auto-ejector can be employed to convince someone to come out of a car when you want to have a friendly neighbor-to-neighbor chat with him after he just hit your bumper. It can also be used to add a little spice to the interior of a car after some jerk has hit your car and walked off, leaving his car locked as a silent reminder of his mindless rampage.

It can also be poked through thin apartment or garage walls with no problem.

When would someone find use for a fogger canister of pepper gas?

Hypothetically speaking, let's say the author had a friend who was asleep in his bed when the neighbors—in this case an office of the local telephone company—decided they should move their equipment to a new facility. As one could expect, the moving crew was fairly unhappy about being drawn from their domicile at 4:30 A.M. so they decided to share this surliness with the occupants of the neighboring houses by throwing glass and furniture, screaming, honking their car horns, and other gestures of goodwill.

Now, my hypothetical friend had a three-month-old baby who had just gone to sleep for his two- to three-hour nap, giving the parents a much needed break, when the merriment began. After several requests from my friend to please quiet down, the offenders began throwing bottles and other objects of refuse into my hypothetical friend's yard and yelling obscenities.

It's just amazing how one small can of pepper gas unobtrusively rolled or thrown into an area of discontent can make the entire environment more harmonious for all persons involved.

And it did.

A HARMLESS ALTERNATIVE

If one wants to produce the visual effect of pepper or tear gas without the follow-up hysteria, it's possible to employ a tactical smoke grenade or the burning "riot buster" smoke grenades that are often used by police for training exercises, war games, and so on.

These units put out approximately 100,000 cubic feet of either white or colored smoke which, though harmless, tends to excite people when thrown into a large boisterous late-night yard party or in or under a vehicle.

Smoke grenades can be purchased from a number of the pyrotechnic suppliers listed in the final chapter of this book.

The terrible trio. **Cap-Stun, Mister Clear Out, and a smoke-producing "riot grenade"—three ways to clear your house of vermin, reposition a Hell's Angels party, or separate the contestants of a small war. All three are legally available by mail order.**

CALCIUM CARBIDE

One of the most versatile compounds known to man is calcium carbide. This chemical is easily obtainable and fun. It comes in gray, rock-like chunks and appears fairly inert while left alone. However, it has an amazing quality that belies its Milquetoast appearance—when calcium carbide is added to water, it reacts violently, releasing acetylene gas.

Acetylene is extremely flammable, explosive if contained, and smells terrible. Before the widespread acceptance of the electric light, calcium carbide was used in miner's helmets, where it was mixed with water in a lamp attached to the front of the helmet. The resulting gas was then burned to give off a bright, white light. Small quantities of calcium carbide produce copious quantities of acetylene.

Perhaps you remember reading the backs of comic books, where they ran ads for a wonderful, neighborhood-shattering invention called "the carbide cannon." This was a little hollow tube that came with a chemical that you added water to and ignited, usually with an electric spark. It produced a very loud bang, equal in strength to a cherry bomb.

The active ingredient in that device was calcium carbide.

What do creative revengists do with calcium carbide? In the past, chemists, engineers, and educated smart asses have been known to use the stuff for all sorts of applications.

Add a quantity of it to a toilet bowl while it is being flushed. The carbide will expand rapidly and cause havoc in the plumbing, possibly breaking pipes.

Put it in the bottom of a washtub or in laundry soap in Laundromats. When it's added to the machine, it will create quite a sensation in the Laundromat and probably cause the owner immense grief.

Add it to water and use it as a poor man's tear gas, forcing the target to hire someone to search his house in an effort to figure out from where the offending odor is originating.

Place quantities of it just under the top layer of dirt in houseplants. When the plants are watered, the target will be quite surprised by the physical reaction and obnoxious smell. Like a cheap horror movie, it will seem like his plants have decided to attack him.

Add it to anything that's going to be added to water, such as floor soap, dishwasher soap, or anything that would go in a bathtub.

Some people have even added calcium carbide to products on store shelves, such as laundry detergents and scrubbing powder, by slipping very small pieces of it through a tiny hole in the box or bag. If done in several stores, this will undoubtedly produce a response that will baffle the manufacturer, who may have to send out representatives or even recall portions of the product to find out what the problem is.

THE SUPER GLUE SHOW

At one time, serious revenge artists employed plastic steel or one of the various epoxy glue compositions on the market to push the limits of their creative envelopes. These substances were used to fill keyholes, fasten doors shut, or otherwise permanently attach objects to other objects that were normally free to go their own ways.

A lot of interesting revenge ideas were conceived and carried out using these substances, but now they are all passé. All of the earlier heavy-duty glues and metal or wood filler pastes had several discouraging features: they were hard to use, required a prolonged setting and drying time, demanded exacting temperatures in order to allow them to dry, and didn't work on everything in a uniform fashion.

As you no doubt know, this has all been revolutionized by a Swedish scientist who discovered super glue. Super glue is available in a number of different consistencies and brands. *Always buy the best!* Some of the cheaper glues do not work as well as the more expensive brands because they are diluted or are not pure.

Super glue sticks virtually anything to virtually anything, works instantly, and provides more strength than most of the materials that are glued together.

To undo the bonding effect of super glue, it is often necessary to break the item rather than destroy the glue bond. One would have to be incredibly dull not to come up with interesting uses for super glue.

Remember, the concept is that things you would normally expect to be mobile are suddenly solid, once-piece units. For instance, various parts on the telephone that you'd expect to be able to push or lift, including push buttons and the handset—with an application of super glue the phone will just ring and ring and ring . . .

Even large items, like a refrigerator, can be sealed with the permanence of a time capsule by the careful application of super glue.

Briefcases, post office boxes, stereo dust covers, cassette decks, VCR deck doors, video-tape boxes, on/off switches on a variety of appliances and electronic equipment, plugs that normally come out of the wall when you yank on them, channel selectors on television remotes, the doors that hold the answering-machine tape in place, book pages, computer disk file boxes, floppy disks that normally turn in order to function, elevator buttons, circuit breakers (that are first turned off), fuses that are replaced in their socket, never to come out again . . .

Whew . . .

Automobiles also offer a variety of tempting targets for the super glue freak. Any lock, from the trunk to the ignition to the gas cap, can be modified into a nonopening feature of the car by gluing the pins or by inserting any small foreign object into the lock and then gluing it in place. Lug nuts can actually be glued onto the wheel, a wonderful stunt that will never be noticed until it comes time to change the tire for one reason or another . . .

Automobile ashtrays can be made completely inoperable, as can cigarette lighters.

Radios can be changed from those obnoxious country and western stations and permanently glued on some good old rock 'n roll. Electric antennas can be unelectricized. Tire caps can be made permanent features of the tire. Cellular telephones can be cemented to their trays. Seat positions can be fixed in place (any place).

Decorative objects can be glued to the outside of vehicles, or signs can be glued onto cars in order to advertise some revealing fact about the target that you think the world has a right to know.

At parties, super glue can create instant hilarity, insuring that everyone has a good time. It can be discreetly applied to the lids of twist-off bottles so they won't. Objects that are carelessly laid on furniture, such as plates or purses, can be made a permanent part of the fixture on which they are resting. If done quickly enough, super glue can be added to objects that someone's about to touch, such as a glass or plate, melding the object and person into harmony.

In fact, the ultimate use of super glue is to glue people to themselves or to their best friends. This is normally accomplished when someone is asleep, drunk, or passed out from some obnoxious chemical they probably shouldn't be using anyway.

Super glue glues flesh as easily as it glues inorganic objects. Hands, feet, ears, and other parts of the anatomy can be creatively and painlessly rearranged into a more pleasing format. By the same token, people sleeping with one or more parts of their body in contact can be encouraged to remain in contact for some time.

On the other end of the spectrum, if you become the victim of anybody who is rotten enough to do any of the above things, remember that super glue is dissolved by acetone, which can be purchased at the drugstore or even at the supermarket in the guise of fingernail polish remover.

MEDICAL/CHEMICAL MAYHEM

There are a number of drugs and chemicals, some prescription and some available over the counter, that cause severe or startling reactions when applied to a target. Needless to say, *never* apply drugs or induce substances into anyone's food or direct environment without a doctor's prescription. To do so would be completely foolhardy and illegal.

MEDICAL MALICE

Every medical student in the country, at least once in his life, has added Pyridium, a commonly available bladder analgesic and antiseptic that is prescribed for infections in this region, and added this tasteless substance to his fellow medical students' food or drink. Pyridium has the side effect of turning one's urine bright red or fluorescent orange, depending on the color of one's urine to begin with.

One tablet is enough to engage this engaging side effect.

Methylene blue is a harmless chemical that turns urine a deep blue.

Ipecac is known as the universal antidote. It's available in a nonprescription form, although most pharmacies now require you to go up to the counter and ask for it rather than stocking it on the shelf.

Ipecac's claim to fame is that it induces immediate vomiting in anyone who swallows a couple drops of it. This is great for forcing a poison victim to disgorge his recent contaminant and terrible for someone who's trying to eat normal food without realizing that it contains this obnoxious chemical.

Antibuse is the alcoholic's answer to electroshock therapy. Antibuse is designed to be consumed by a chronic alcoholic with the full knowledge that if it's followed by a single drink containing alcohol, the person will become sick immediately.

There's no law that says you have to be an alcoholic to get a taste of this stuff. If it is mixed in food and followed by an alcoholic drink, the results are much the same.

Inexplicable and instant.

Several common substances do the exact opposite of antibuse and Ipecac. They create diarrhea. The most widely known of these is dish soap. If dish soap residue remains on eating utensils or in food, it will trigger diarrhea. So will substances designed to do this, such as castor oil, heavy laxatives, and, oddly enough, a few drops of hydraulic fluid.

Diarrhea at its extreme can be propagated by a couple drops of horse laxative, which can be purchased without a prescription at veterinary supply houses. The taste of horse laxative can be fairly strong and fairly chemical in makeup, so it's usually mixed with something that will overwhelm one's taste buds, like chocolate-covered cherries.

An interesting sidebar on the diarrhea-inducing concept was engineered by a friend of mine (*another* friend) who, after having his food repeatedly stolen from his college dorm room, decided to coat some homemade chocolate chip cookies with a tasty frosting of melted Ex-Lax.

The perp spent the next couple days in his room with the door locked, and the food theft ceased immediately.

In old-time detective movies, someone is always slipping "knockout drops" into somebody else's drink. These are normally central nervous system depressants that have a cross-tolerance with alcoholic beverages. The most common is chloral hydrate. Although it has a slightly bitter taste, it is usually concealed in any alcoholic drink that contains fruit and/or sugar.

Chloral hydrate induces sleep and functions well with alcohol to literally knock a person out.

Largactyl is a sleep inducer that is used as a knockout drop when mixed with normal (non-alcoholic) food. It takes two to four tablets to make most people drowsy and eventually escape into somnambulism.

Itching powder, the dream of all comic book classified readers, really is available. Old-fashioned, real, make-them-itch-til . . .

This still works. If you happen to know a very passive tarantula and you have a pair of small, sharp scissors . . .

A more practical substitute is fiberglass filaments from insulation. They produce a rash and itch like hell.

Dimethyl sulfoxide, or DMSO, is a liquid with a unique property—if you mix it with any other liquid, or a solid chemical that will dissolve it, and it's touched by flesh, it will penetrate the flesh and enter the bloodstream in a matter of seconds.

DMSO mixed with lemon juice, tear gas, pepper, hallucinogenic drugs, vinegar, or any other number of tasteful items can be "injected" into a target's bloodstream by lacing a door-knob or steering wheel with the mixture.

It normally takes about thirty seconds from touching the chemical combination until it reaches the victim's taste buds.

CHEMICAL COMBOS

Without necessitating a master's degree in organic chemistry, there are a number of ways household substances can be harnessed to provide power for the serious revengist's motor.

Some household cleaning chemicals will react when mixed together. A good example of this is the combination of Sani-Flush (sodium bisulfate) and Comet (sodium hypochlorite). When combined in the presence of water, chlorine gas is released under a fair bit of pressure. Although outlawed by the Geneva Convention for use in war, leaving layers of these chemicals where they will be exposed to water, such as a dishwasher, can provide interesting results. If the combination is put in a toilet tank, the pressure may actually make it explode.

Sodium silicate, commonly called water glass, is a rather inert, viscous liquid that resembles a thick syrup. When it is exposed to air for a lengthy period, it dries into a very hard substance resembling glass. If the liquid is placed on things, especially on glass, it will dry and bond onto the material, leaving an unusual residue that's almost impossible to remove.

Things that smell like rotten eggs include hydrogen sulfide, which can be purchased at most scientific supply houses, often in a small container that will react when heated to give off a characteristic gas. Ammonium sulfate is another substance that has a generally rotten smell. If aluminum foil is mixed with hydrochloric acid, it produces potentially flammable and explosive hydrogen gas as well as other gases that smell extremely raunchy.

On the more exciting side of things, sodium metal (which is extremely dangerous to handle) reacts violently when dropped in water. This reaction includes bursting into flames, vaporizing the water, skipping around, and generally creating mayhem. Very interesting in an enclosed area such as a swimming pool or jacuzzi.

As long as we're on the subject of jacuzzis, a tablet of Salvo bubbles wonderfully when fed through the water pump system. Red dye does a fair job of turning things a different hue. Dye markers that are designed to be thrown into water for emergency situations provide an even deeper staining power (you can pick these up at surplus stores).

Silver nitrate (used to cauterize wounds, among other things) stains anything it touches dark brown or black. The stain is extremely difficult to remove. Some people mix silver nitrate with soap bars, shampoos, or skin cleaners that are to be used directly by the target.

CORPORATE TAKEDOWNS

BANKS

At sometime or another in every person's life, he is going to be mistreated by a bank. That's just the way it is. Not to put all banks down or say that all bank personnel are terrible people, but sooner or later, you will run up against one that is.

For reasons unknown—maybe a change in personnel or a policy shift to discourage small investors and concentrate services only on large corporate investors who form the bulk of their income—you will be treated flat-out shoddily by a bank.

This treatment may come in various forms, including large service fees for storing your money, transaction fees, inability or no incentive to add your statement correctly, no follow-through on anything, or simply bad service in general.

Everyone dreams about getting even with giant corporations through some devious little trick that will bring them to their knees. If it were that easy, there would be a lot of corporations—and lots of banks in particular—kissing the ground.

There are a few things you can do to at least cost a bank some money and time keeping tabs on your personal finances. The simplest trick is to write your checks in what is known as nonreproducible blue ink. Pens full of nonrepro blue ink can be purchased at any graphic art supply store. They're used for marking documents that are going to be sent to an offset printer.

Printing cameras are specifically designed to be insensitive to light-blue ink. This allows corrections and notations to be made on the about-to-be-printed copy without the camera picking them up and reproducing them. Nonrepro blue ink does not like to be photographed by regular cameras, nor does it particularly liked to be photocopied.

Banks like to take pictures of your checks. They like to photocopy checks. If you ask them for copies of your recent checks because you disagree with their bookkeeping, they will have to try to photocopy the nonrepro blue, which is not easy.

Banks also hold onto your checks approximately two years (or more) in the form of microfilm. This is for the convenience of anyone who comes calling, such as the IRS, Franchise Tax Board, or any other member of the government with their palms outspread.

It's possible to buy nonmicrofilm pens that have a deep purple-red ink. This color is just flat-out impossible to microfilm and will drive anyone trying to do so crazy.

A simpler technique to delay correct debiting on your checking account and generally screw up any kind of automatic accounting system is to look at the account and bank numbers on your checks.

If they are printed magnetically—that is, if they are printed with magnetic ink, as many checks are—you can run the checks one by one over a tape demagnetizer or rub them on a strong magnet. If you don't have a strong magnet just lying about waiting for checks to be rubbed on it, use the magnet on any large hi-fi speaker. This will scramble the information on your checks, making the magnetic readers unable to function. Your checks will have to be fed in one at a time by hand.

If the checks are optically numbered, it is possible to take a razor blade and scrape one or more of the individual account numbers away to arrive at the same effect.

Be advised that the bank is not going to take this kind of treatment forever, and they have the option of asking you to take your money elsewhere. The more money you have in your account, the less likely they will be to do this, but eventually any bank will get tired of seeing nonrepro blue ink or checks that mysteriously won't go through their machines.

At this point they will close out your account. This is legal. There's not much you can do about it, so bear this in mind when you decide to tamper with your own checks.

Now if you were to tamper with other people's checks . . .

The ultimate way to get even with a bank would be to withdraw a large amount of cash that wasn't yours. This would not only injure the institution but would probably help your life-style to some degree. However, be aware that the FBI does not want to hear stories of how badly the bank treated you if you are arrested for robbing a bank or for fraud. This is a very real risk. *We do not advise anyone to do anything to a bank or institution.* The items discussed here are only to acquaint you with what has gone on in the past and what people are doing and how to better protect your funds.

ATM MACHINES

ATM machines are often considered the weak point of any banking institution (for good reasons) and there are numerous ways to screw with them, either by messing things up or extracting money that isn't yours.

Approximately 45,000 ATM machines were in use by the end of 1989. In addition, about one-fifth of the nation's 18,000 banks belong to 100 ATM regional fund-transfer networks.

Approximately one dozen U.S. banks have more than 2,000 ATM machines per corporation. Each machine sells for about $30,000. Ninety-five percent of banks not using ATMs currently expect to incorporate them into their systems in the next five years. Burroughs, NCR, Docutel, Diebold, and IBM are among the largest manufacturers of ATMs.

The majority of ATMs are attached directly to the dispensing bank and are called "through-the-wall" ATMs. The other style is known as "stand-alone" and is used mainly in shopping malls, convention centers, hospitals, hotels, and transportation facilities.

There are many uses for ATMs, including withdrawals, deposits, interbank transfers, transfers between savings and checking accounts, and getting information on accounts.

ATM use will continue to grow in the future.

Accounts accessed through ATMs can be protected by a secret PIN (personal identification number) and PIN transformations (all ATMs), PIN and/or data encryption (about 25 percent), message authentication (about 10 percent), secure-line (all through-the-walls, some stand-alones), maximum withdrawal limits (all, on a daily basis), and automatic card confiscation (all ATMs).

Data gathered in 1988 from sixteen American banks showed a median loss from ATM fraud of $84 million.

The maximum amount of cash ATMs hold is usually $50,000. Some bank security departments file ATMs away as a low-level risk when compared to other banking vulnerabilities such as electronic corporate fund transfers, where huge amounts are changed in one transaction.

Security should, but often doesn't, extend beyond the vulnerability of the cash ATMs contain. The machines are located in extremely high-traffic areas, which opens a path for PIN code acquisition as well as cons and muggings.

The objective of an ATM site selection is to attract and keep a large number of customers. Inadequate or poor planning in choosing sites can make the best security efforts fall short.

The trend today is for banks to allow customers to apply debit cards from one bank's ATM installations to another through interconnecting systems. Security does not seem to have kept pace with this growth.

The fraudulent use of ATM codes and cards presents a big problem. As better electronic means are developed to attack current security measures, the present surveillance equipment will not be good enough.

To help minimize risks on electronic fund transfers and protect the machines and users at individual ATMs, banks should provide the following at ATM locations:

- minimal furnishings
- good lighting
- access control
- good visibility
- alarm systems
- telephone
- closed-circuit TV
- phony alarm and FBI decals

Camera surveillance of the area helps prevent vandalism, which has been a large problem with ATM machines. The closed-circuit TV cameras are often activated when a card is inserted.

One obvious weak point is that ATMs belonging to small banks are not as sturdy as is commonly expected. Larger banks, such as Wells Fargo or Bank of America, use much sturdier construction.

The money safe in Diebold-made ATMs is not tool resistant or burglarproof, but is usually only fire resistant. It may even have wheels on the bottom. Most ATMs are not physically secured very well and could be ripped out by a large truck. Robbers could break the glass and wrap a chain around the unit, pulling it free.

Some banks print out each ATM transaction on an on-line printer and flag any suspicious ones. All through-the-wall ATMs are on-line to parent computers, while stand-alones can be either off-line or on-line.

The bank side of through-the-wall ATMs usually has camera controls along with the date and time LED display information, but frequent errors in time occur, which would make the photos inaccurate, providing alibis for the user.

It is often possible for someone inside the bank to reach the ATM controls and change them, as they are usually in public areas.

Beating an obvious camera is easy: simply block the view with a newspaper, piece of cardboard, or aluminum foil.

Spray paint, paintballs, or thick liquids can defeat the camera's usefulness, as can a bright light.

Experts have discovered that customers feel safe and secure at an ATM if they are visible from the street. If the device is hidden in a vestibule, the entire area should be lit with 100- to 150-foot candles, with no blinds, drapes, or other coverings over the glass areas. To help eliminate natural blind spots, mirrors can be installed.

Both vestibules or through-the-wall ATMs in a financial service office should always be well-lit and free of other structures or shrubbery that could hide a potential attacker.

Access should only be through one door made of solid wood or hollow metal that only opens through the service area. There should be a wide-angle peephole to allow people to view the exterior before opening the enclosure door.

Alarm protection should include the following:

- Complete electric lining or wrapping of all six interior sides of the money chest, or a state-of-the-art vibration detector.

- A contact switch to sense when the money chest is open.

- The ability to detect a thermal attack.

- A detector switch on each combination lock to monitor whether the boltwork is locked or unlocked.

Lack of any of these security measures leaves an opening for both vandalism and theft. Thieves have been known to drill and burn into the machines, pull the cash dispenser loose, and even blow them apart with dynamite.

A really neat, quick trick utilizes liquid nitrogen. It is poured onto the ATM, freezing the unit to about -100 degrees. Then it is smashed with a sledge or large ball-peen hammer, shattering the crystallized metal. The burglar then is able to reach in and grab whatever he wants.

It is possible to replace or modify ATMs by surreptitiously installing a false front (or doing so while dressed as a bank or ATM employee), but it must be done properly if it is to look legitimate and be able to fool bank personnel. A false front could be glued on or attached with two-sided tape.

People have also employed false extensions that extend about one inch from the real ATM card slot. They have a built-in skimmer that detects and transmits the encrypted PINs while the actual PIN entries are being processed.

A variation of this is to install another type of false front over the buttons and record the actual PIN entries as they are punched in.

Nothing pisses a bank off more than to lose money, customers, and face if this sort of trick is made public.

It's also within the realm of reason to utilize a full false front that covers the entire ATM and extends out four to six feet. Such false-front (or "privately owned") ATMs "borrow" the real machine's buttons and intake slot but provide their own holding bin for outgoing cash.

Three-day holiday weekends make for good application periods. When a user attempts to make a withdrawal, the cash is detoured over to the holding bin and the readout indicates a bad card. Any PIN entry is also recorded on cassette.

The perpetrator then grabs the cash and uses the PINs to make withdrawals at other, real ATMs. The false fronts are destroyed at the end of the weekend.

Some ATMs use money drawers. A really clever thief will tape or epoxy the drawer closed, return at the end of a weekend, remove the tape or shatter the epoxy with a hammer, and leave with the stash.

ATMs that use money slots can be blocked up with glue or part of a folded black index card, causing the money to jam and collect at the exit slot until the machine malfunctions.

Does this work in real life? A man covering his face stole about $70,000 from a Wells Fargo Bank ATM in San Leandro, California, by jamming it with a bank card covered with glue.

Many banks, such as First Interstate, realize that the problem exists but choose to ignore it.

They argue against adding ATM protection with closed-circuit TVs because they have not been able to justify the cost of such installations for their systems. ATMs do not present a big enough risk in their eyes. The expense of the additional equipment might not cover the losses it would prevent. Banks accept a degree of risk and loss and often find basic security measures to be sufficient.

Many banks economize by using fake closed-circuit TVs at ATMs. These nonoperative cameras act as a deterrent to thieves without the expense of a real film operation.

Through-the-wall ATMs are not as great a security risk during servicing as free-standing machines. Servicing is done within the bank by in-house staff in a secure environment. It is more difficult to service free-standing units.

Despite the method a bank has agreed upon for ATM servicing, certain basic security guidelines continue to be the same. An essential component is the use of a quality ATM alarm system capable of differentiating among signals. Also, all ATM servicing (such as alarm-system deactivation or general machine entry) should be watched while it's in progress. A keypad alarm control with antiambush features is another necessary strong feature. *But most banks don't bother with this level of protection.*

ATMs should be serviced as quickly as possible to reduce exposure. Bank management should try not to resupply an ATM after hours but should do so during the day instead. Yet many are serviced during high-risk hours.

FRAUD

In addition to the physical and operational problems of protecting the ATM is the complex problem of fraud. Fraud is oh-so-difficult to prove, and due to the Federal Reserve Board's

Regulation E, which protects the customers, the burden of proof is entirely on the bank. Reg. E, known as the Electronics Funds Transfer Act of 1979, was passed by Congress to protect customers from losses by mistakes of electronic transfers of funds. Customers are only minimally liable for acts that result in loss to a bank. This amount is limited to fifty dollars.

Unless a bank can prove conclusively that a customer authorized the transfer of funds or actually performed a fraudulent transaction, *the customer is not liable*. In a fraud case, the security manager must prove the perpetrator guilty or discover who actually made the fraudulent transactions.

Besides a physical attack on an ATM, criminal activity against a bank falls into the following categories: unauthorized card use, fraudulent card use, insider manipulation, embezzlement, robbery, and mugging

The Electronic Funds Transfer Act defines an unauthorized electronic fund transfer as ". . . a transfer from a consumer's account initiated by a person other than the consumer without actual authority to initiate such transfer and from which the consumer receives no benefit." Unauthorized transfers can be initiated through ATM access cards.

How? Thieves often obtain cards by stealing purses or wallets. Many customers, despite all financial institutions advising against it, keep a record of their personal identification number (PIN) with their cards, which enables thieves easy access to the customer's account.

On the other hand, it is difficult to prove an unauthorized transaction if a friend or family member steals a customer's card, knows the PIN, and makes a withdrawal without the owner knowing. The card is then returned surreptitiously to its owner. When charges appear on the statement and it is disputed, the victim insists the card was never out of his possession. The burden of proof is on the financial institution.

Counterfeit access cards are another method of performing unauthorized transfers. Visa and MasterCards are often used for this type of transaction, but the use of counterfeit ATM cards is increasing.

Skimming is another interesting get-even crime committed by a perpetrator who has access to credit or debit cards (i.e., waiters, cashiers, gas-pump operators). He simply passes a magnetic-strip reader over the debit card's magnetic strip. Skimmers can either be homemade or purchased. Or he can do one of the following:

1) A piece of cassette or video tape is positioned over the magnetic strip on the back of the card. A clothes iron or soldering iron is heated to 300 degrees and rubbed against the tape. The tape picks up the recorded information. It is then placed over a blank tape cemented to the back of a counterfeit card and ironed down, transferring the information to the counterfeit card.

Like magic . . .

2) A strip of chromium dioxide is placed over the magnetic strip and a hot iron rubbed against it. The encrypted data is then visibly transferred to the chromium dioxide strip without harming the original information on the card.

3) A simple digital "read head" is electronically connected to a digital "write head." The read head is skimmed over the magnetic strip while the write head simultaneously reproduces the encrypted data on a strip of cassette tape.

These devices are readily available from many large electronic retailers and can be salvaged (with electronics) from cassette recorders, disk drives, or similar equipment.

4) A magnetic strip reader is purchased. Its output is recorded and/or transferred to a magnetic card writer. A bogus card can then be encrypted immediately. This will piss off the bank as well as the cardholder, *although the bank will be responsible for any illegal withdrawal.*

5) Here's a home brew, techie, "Gee, Mr. Wizard!" trick. Scatter very fine iron filings over the magnetic strip. They will arrange themselves to show the encrypted data as in a physical photo.

How are fraudulent cards used? A customer can make an electronic fund transfer and then disagree when it appears on his statement. According to Regulation E, if the financial institution cannot prove the disputed transaction was made with the owner's knowledge, it must reimburse the customer.

The correct generation and use of ATM cards and personal identification numbers are supposed to be a security priority.

PINs can combine customer-chosen codes with bank-selected numbers that are both passed through an algorithmic equation to arrive at the true PIN. Therefore, the number that passes through the system is not the same one the customer punches into the machine. If the PIN is intercepted outside the ATM, the numbers entered by the customer at the ATM are not the same as those received at the host computer. Even this is not a foolproof method, as we'll see . . .

Encryption is a major part of data security. With this system, a normal message is altered to arrive as a new message less intelligible to the receiver or anyone else along the line. Only the processing computer knows the key and is able to decipher and translate the message.

A process known as "spoofing" circumvents encryption by ignoring it and duplicating the code sequence. In a usual sequence, two individuals—one at the ATM and the other on-line—locate the signal being sent and decide how it looks when the money is dispensed. Once a pattern is ferreted out, the person at the ATM can inquire about a balance, but the message routed back can be changed to inform the ATM to dispense cash.

PIN Numbers

The clear PIN is the nonencrypted PIN you chose or the bank chooses for you. An example of a clear PIN would be 8764.

The encrypted PIN is a clear PIN that is changed to an unrecognizable form by an algorithm. The encrypted version of 8764 might be 2895.

In most cases, the bank uses an encrypted PIN in its debit account file. This is a reference PIN and is used to verify PINs entered into its ATMs. An encrypted PIN can also be used on the debit card's magnetic strip.

The key to defeating ATMs is to acquire both the clear and encrypted PINs as used on the magnetic strips.

Most magnetic strips consist of three tracks: TK1, TK2, and TK3. TK1 and TK2 are read-only tracks while TK3 can be read or written to.

TK1 is the only encrypted track that contains the encrypted cardholder's name, thus permitting the customer's name to be inexpensively printed on ATM receipts (in this system the name does not have to be gathered from the host computer).

The American Bankers Association funded the development of TK2 for Interbank and Visa. Their intention was to develop a standardized card for use with terminals to authorize credit card transactions.

TK2 is the most popular encryption method for plastic cards. It is widely used by banks because most ATMs need a common system to allow standard computer accessing. It is the preferred choice of the ABA, and is the only track supported and recognized by MasterCard and Visa in both their debit and credit card systems.

How do smart folks get PINs? One method relies on the fact that each key on a keypad has a slightly different sound when it is used, even if you can't detect these differences by ear.

The outlaw uses one FM transmitter. He feeds the detected audio into an A/D converter and then into a signal analyzer. He makes a voice print analysis for each key's sound. Then he can determine which keys were used.

Another trick that has been used with some success is to videotape the transaction from a nearby van using a telephoto lens.

SOCIAL NETWORKING

Be aware that ninety-five percent of all ATM fraud can be attributed to the fraudulent use of the consumer's card by an acquaintance or another family member. Knowing this is one thing, proving it is quite another, especially without a photograph, fingerprints, or witness . . .

Most banks won't bother . . .

SOCIAL ENGINEERING AND PEOPLE PHREAKING

A number of years ago I stood next to a man who was probably the best known "phone phreak" in the world and watched him employ a technique known as "social engineering" to cost one of the world's largest corporations untold millions of dollars.

He did it in about 4 minutes . . .

At that time AT&T issued "credit card" numbers to any subscriber, which allowed him to charge calls anywhere, no questions asked, as long as they could give the operator the proper credit card number.

The magic number included the customer's telephone number and a randomly generated computer code that was changed every six months for security purposes (both to invalidate the number in case it had fallen into the wrong hands as well as to cancel the service for people who did not pay their bills to the phone company's satisfaction).

Because computers were not sophisticated enough to make it cost effective to verify every single request (they had to be manually entered, among other problems), the code was in fact an algorithm that could eventually be cracked. The six month time period was also a method of discouraging people from putting too much time into breaking a code, as it would soon be obsolete.

My friend knew that a new code had been generated and was just about to be given out to the various computer centers around the company. He called the San Francisco office and asked for a certain VP (whose name he knew quite well) during lunch hour and got the man's secretary on the line.

He identified himself as Mr. XXX, president of security for AB&C Phone Company and demanded to speak to the VP.

Impossible, the woman said.

Well, it was imperative he be located because an important security matter was at stake.

She didn't know where he was. Could the call be returned?

No, he had to verify that their office had received the new supersecret computer codes for the credit card system. Did she know if in fact they had received this information?

"Uh, sorry. I'm not allowed to discuss those matters without prior . . ."

"Young lady," my friend said, "do you like your job?"

"Yes, I do."

"Do you have any idea who I am?"

"Well, no I don't." (Damn right she didn't!)

"I'm going to tell you who I am and exactly what you have to do in order to keep your job. Listen closely . . ."

This conversation ended with him directing her to dig around on her boss's desk in order to find the envelope from "his" security office.

She found it.

"Fine. You're doing fine. Now I need to verify that you were sent the right instructions. A number of incorrect letters were mailed. Rip the envelope open and read me what it says."

"Should I read the part about not giving this information to anyone, even phone company employees, too?"

"Yes. Read it all."

She did. And several weeks before the legitimate phone company employees got the new codes, several thousand hackers and bulletin board members had the information necessary to convert any phone number into a valid credit card code.

The next six months set a record for fraudulent credit card calls . . .

Every corporation is a system. It's possible to use this system against itself by understanding a little bit about the way it works and its vulnerable points. One can use the personality of the system to thrash it.

DUMPSTER DIVING

This is an actual technique employed in industrial espionage that works well in get-even schemes. Much of the data that is grabbed surreptitiously from corporations *is retrieved from their trash bins.*

Many corporations treat their garbage as just that—garbage. True hackers and phreaks consider it a gold mine.

In many cases it is possible to simply drive around to the rear of a building and "dive" into the trash. It can also be bagged up for later examination.

What can one glean from this type of fishing trip? Memos, names, customers, phone numbers, passwords, ways in, ways out, sources of information, and starting points.

A few companies have learned, the hard way, to at least lock up their trash, but this is usually involves a padlock and easily cut chain at best.

Some corporations will go so far as to add a security guard. Does this guarantee security? Guards are normally low-paid, blue-collar workers *who have access to any secure area.*

By adding a guard, a company may have actually lowered its security. How do people take advantage of this situation?

One method is to get an old shopping cart and dress up like a homeless person. Approach the guard. Hold out a bag of aluminum cans and ask, "Can I go in the trash to look for old cans? I have a kid at home and he needs food."

Often the security guard will put his master key in the lock and open it. Suddenly it's easier to get into the target trash bin with that security guard there then when it was "just" protected by a steel fence.

Corporations spend millions of dollars on hardware to protect their ideas and then they completely compromise everything with a little foolishness.

Dumpster diving is like being invited into the front door to help yourself to just about anything you want. Even simple memos will establish the chain of command, tell you who issues what kind of orders, and give you a starting place for creative memos and phone calls.

Corporate officers, department heads, officers from branch offices—find out their name or even their secretary's name and one can call the personnel department and say, "Hi, this is Bill, Mr. Stevens's executive assistant. He needs some information on employee number XXX . . ."

Why does this work? Why would a complete stranger give an anonymous voice potentially damaging information?

Because most business personnel, no matter what their job title is, are not trained to be security conscious.

Secretaries and low-level management are usually going to be more than willing to give whatever information you want because the corporation works better when people cooperate. The public front is one of helpfulness. A personnel clerk's attitude is rarely one of, "When I pick up the phone, is somebody going to try to get data he is not supposed to get?"

No, his job is to be helpful to people that need this data. How can they look better in their job? A vice president wants something; here's a chance to distinguish oneself in front of heavy management.

You can tighten this entire process by doing a bit of creative fine tuning. First, everything is *urgent.* Reports are always needed right away. Politely ask for an estimate of the time required to fulfill your request. Get an exact time frame, then call back to make certain they received the request and if indeed the material is ready.

How to safely get the material? Should the secretary send it over? No. Your boss needs the info so badly he'll send a messenger . . .

Now the choices are many, from using a real messenger or Federal Express person (which will leave a paper trail), or get your own Fed Ex uniform . . .

Not that hard to do. All this started with one purloined memo and a couple of names.

What if the company is hip enough to call back and verify such requests? All is not lost. Many electronic phone systems, such as ROLM, have a feature known as remote call forwarding. With the proper system handbook, one can have any phone on the system forwarded to another number.

Normally there is no indication that this feature is in use. If the calls are forwarded to a "clean" number, someone answers and verifies the request. Other calls are then answered and switched back to the legit extension until the remote feature can be disabled.

The same leverage can be adapted to military operations. If PFC Williams is working in the data center when Specialist Johnson calls to ask why General Stevens can't have certain information, chances are the info will be given out.

In fact, because of the military concept that one should never question an order, PFC Williams will become intimidated and helpful, especially if someone demands his name and serial number.

Another oft-dumped treasure consists of computer disks. What happens when a floppy disk dies or produces some sort of error message?

You throw it out, of course. If it contains what you feel is valuable information, you erase it first. If you think you're really hip, you reformat it, which destroys all information. Right?

Not true. Most disks that have been machine erased or reformatted still contain much of the data on the disk. There are a number of companies that make a living from recovering this "lost" data.

They advertise in computer magazines . . .

A more dangerous method of obtaining illicit information, computer codes, passwords, memos, and so on is to take a fishing trip. If the security is poor at a certain office, hook on a tool belt and pose as a technician, phone installer, or other "piece of furniture" type and then fish around . . .

SOCIAL ENGINEERING

Feel an urge to attend parties or maybe live theater, even though someone thoughtlessly left you off of the guest list? Here's one system that has worked in the past.

Go down to the theater and look around for the backdoor to the stage.

Right before the event is going to begin, call up the arena. Under normal circumstances the box office will answer. Request a transfer to security at the stage door on the corner of XXX and YYY. Then come on strong as John Smith with Filmore West Productions. Guest what?

There are a couple of last-minute names to be added to the guest list.

Tell the nice gentleman to add "your name here" plus one to the list. This will allow you and any last-minute guest you meet (or your wife, of course) to get in and receive VIP treatment. A nice little extra touch would be to also put the new names on the backstage pass and party list.

See how the other half lives, get good seats, scarf down free booze, feed your family, impress your friends.

On a more serious note, the same technique can be applied to corporate functions. Use those little pieces of information you've gleaned from your purloined memos . . .

USING ONE OFFICE AGAINST ANOTHER

This, as they say, is a true story. It is basically a harmless prank, but it illustrates an important principle in corporate manipulations.

A few years back a certain fast-food franchise was doing one of their periodic game piece giveaways. Collect the pieces and win a fortune . . .

Needless to say, far more tacos are given away than $10,000 checks, but still, one's chances go up in direct proportion to the number of game pieces available . . .

Some people decided that they would like to play the game. One member called the company's national headquarters and located a major franchisee in the New York area. Posing as a potential franchise purchaser, he was given the name of a gentleman who owned eight outlets in the area.

It's common practice between stores that are owned by the same franchisee to share supplies. If the stash of taco sauce gets low, call up a brother store and say, "We need some sauce and don't get a delivery until tomorrow. Can I borrow some? I'll send a kid over to pick it up."

The group chose seven of the eight stores and made the eighth the "store in need." They acquired a uniform, called each of the stores, and said, "Listen. We are running out of game tickets. We aren't getting a delivery until tomorrow. Can you spare a box?"

Figure 10,000 tickets in each box times seven turned into a hell of a lot of free food and a couple of $1,000 checks . . .

In summary, all the hardware in the world will not protect a system if there is a human element involved. People can be bribed, cajoled, or socially engineered to give access to systems and valuable information.

As more people get involved, it becomes a logarithmic equation of possibilities.

COMPUTER PASSWORDS

Most computer programs are protected by a password. Said password blocks unauthorized entry and prevents outsiders from accessing or changing data stored in any of the computer's memory facilities. In theory, a password is almost perfect protection because, depending on the number and type of characters used, it can require years of superfast computer time to break. Or it can be, quite frankly, unbreakable with the correct protection.

This is good if you are involved in computers, because the password can be the key to horrendously effective revenge schemes, including the placement of bombs and horses, data theft and changes, and unauthorized use of computer facilities.

Companies have literally been forced into bankruptcy because someone was careless with one password.

A password lets even a computer-illiterate person into the system. Most friendly systems provide help menus and directories to guide one around the system and help accomplish whatever is wished. A password is *gold*.

But if passwords are so difficult to crack, why do we include them here?

Because most of them really are not that difficult to dig out. There are a number of things many passwords have in common, the most important being that the selector selects a password with some sort of meaning or association that makes it easy to remember. This is the basis on which many passwords are hacked.

In a recent study of thousands of computer systems, it was discovered that many passwords fall into two categories. The first group included the first name of the operator, his spouse, his children, any of their initials, or on occasion, their surname.

To attack these, ascertain who the highest executives in a company are. Include the system operator, head engineer, maintenance engineer, and system installer. Frequently, when a system is being set up and people are being trained to use it, the installer will use Mr. Big

Shot's name as a password. If you find this sort of "backdoor" password, you will find others have been left hanging around as well.

Another technique is to ferret out the interests of the top personnel in the company and try passwords that pertain to these interests.

Such information is frequently published in local newspapers, is available from the company, or can be found in the public library or through business clubs. Search through the trash if at all possible. Nicknames, home addresses, SSNs, phone numbers, and addresses are also popular passwords. Social Security numbers seem to be a favorite of many users and may be acquired by procuring a person's credit report or by paying a minor charge (usually about one dollar) to the Department of Motor Vehicles to get registered ownership information of any particular vehicle.

The second huge category of password names comes from—surprise—the subject's environment! That means his computer system. The most common password in the world today is—guess what?—PASSWORD!

Yes, that's true. When a computer program prompts a user to come up with a password, in a salute to the creativity of the American public (those same people who put their initials on their custom license plates), many choose the word "password."

There are many other computer-oriented passwords, including: PEEK, DIAG, DIAGNOSTIC, HELP, DISK, TEST, TESTER, TESTING, SYSTEM, SYSTEM MANAGER, SYS, SYSMAN, SECTOR, SYSOP, SYSMAN, HELLO, ENGINEER, OPS, OPERATIONS, PHONE, GUEST, CENTRAL, SECRET, TOP SECRET, MODEM, IBMCE, LOVE, SEX (and the many synonyms for sex), DATA, DEMO, DEMONSTRATION, MICRO, POKE, LOOP, GIGO, AID, DISPLAY, BYTE, CALL, CIPHER, TERMINAL, TERM, EXTERNAL, BAUD, REMOTE, CHECK, NET, NETWORK, FRED, CONFIG, CONFIGURE, AND ZEUS.

Passwords are mainly one or two words. If they are two words, they are frequently separated by a period (".") or question mark ("?"). Word format and the delimiter chosen depends upon the system itself.

Each password is at least three characters in length. In a one-word system, the length is often, six, eight, or ten characters. In a two-word system, ten to twelve characters is the most popular format, though the words are often common and easily spelled.

114

Letters are usually upper case and may be used with numbers.

Numbers are often used alone, in which case punctuation, graphics, or graphic characters are seldom interjected in order to complicate things.

Remember, people tend to reuse passwords. One that worked on another system or has been used before may still be valid on a new system.

System and company booklets are a fine starting place. All systems include password examples. A number of these set-up passwords are never changed and are still in operation. System manuals can be acquired from the manufacturer, computer bookstores, or libraries.

This situation creates what is known as "trap door" or "backdoor" passwords—passwords which exist outside the system operator's domain. They may have been put there by the company that developed the software, by a technician who installed it, someone who worked on it, or by someone who simply wanted to make sure he had a way into the system in case of trouble.

Backdoor passwords are often things like: HELP, GUEST, and IBMCE. If you find one of these backdoor passwords, you have stumbled onto especially good news since they will often bypass all other security levels.

It's also wise to try AAAA or words that are easily typed on a typewriter keyboard for those lazy or hunt-and-peck typers out there. These words include: QWERKY, FRED, and ASDFG.

If the password is numeric, sequential strings such as 12345678 and easily typed quickies like 101010 or 11111111, 22222222, etc., have worked many times, surprising sophisticated hackers who expect to be faced with much higher security in these systems.

If the password syntax is numeric, the second most obvious things to try are birthdays, phone numbers, vehicle license numbers, bank account numbers, addresses, anniversaries, ages, children's ages, and so on.

Besides the operator, there's also a fair shot if one can discover the name of the top exec in the organization, the CEO, or any vice president. Try his name, nicknames, or those of his children, because there's a very good chance that when the system was set up, it was demonstrated to him, probably with a tech rep on the premises. Quick access with his own choice of password was probably offered to make the system seem extremely simple.

This word may still be a valid entry.

A good method to obtain passwords is through physical inspection: the would-be penetrator gets access to a facility with computer terminals and finds passwords taped on the computer or printed on paper in trash receptacles. People who work at home most often have their IDs and passwords taped to their computers, since they think they are protected in this location. It is also possible to watch someone using a computer terminal to see what they type as a password, even though it does not show on the screen.

Another easy method of obtaining passwords is to find a helper who is employed at the company the hacker hopes to penetrate. Obviously, that person can supply needed answers to questions about the computer system being used by the target company.

Passwords can sometimes be obtained by tricking the user to show them. An on-line session can be interrupted through a "chat" or "conference" mode, wherein a hacker pretends to be a system operator and requests that the user re-enter his password.

In fact, more often than you would think, one can simply write a person a letter and say, "Hi, I'm a computer hacker freak whom your company has grossly offended and I feel retribution is in order. Would you please be so kind as to give me your password so I can go in and mess up your computer files, steal your customers, harass your secretaries and terminal operators, and generally wreck your company. Sincerely yours, XXX."

Remember, always be polite.

Sound silly? No. This works more often than you think. The only adjustment is that you have to fine-tune your letter:

The idea is to ask, "Would you please tell me your password? I need it badly," in a way which can't be refused . . .

THE LETTER

June 19, 1990

Dr. H. Hacker
1234 Elm Street
Cleveland, OH 80212

Victim of your heinous plot
Large Conglomerate and Extortion Company, Inc.
666 Avenue of the Americas
New York, NY 10011

Dear Sir:

I'm with the security department of (Dialog, One-line, CompuServe, Local Area Network, *MacWinner* magazine, *Computer Security Newsletter*, etc.), and it has become apparent to us that the incidents of password hacking—unauthorized users determining the structure and content of passwords in order to bypass legitimate security—is on the rise in your type of system. It is my job to help eliminate these breaches of computer security by increasing the security of your password system.

I would greatly appreciate your completing and returning to me the enclosed form. The results of our studies will enhance both corporate and personal security and be a major benefit to users like yourself.

Thank you for your time and consideration.

Dr. H. Hacker
V.P. Security

THE FORM

A SECURITY SURVEY OF XXX PASSWORDS

1. Relationship between the symbols of your password:

   a. Does your password contain two letters that are the same?

   yes   no

   b. Does your password contain two numbers that are the same?

   yes   no

2. Structure of passwords:

   Please indicate with a cross the position of the letters in your password.

   –––––––––

3. Is the first symbol in your password a zero?

   yes   no

4. Letters making up your password:

   Please provide, in alphabetical order, the sequence of letters making up your password?

5. Address of other people using the service:

Please fold this form, staple it, and return.

Thank you for your cooperation.

COMPUTER VIRUSES

Most public articles suggest that the ability to create a virus resides only in rocket scientists or top-level programmers.

This is a lie.

Viruses have come to mean any kind of computer program that has a negative function.

The most widespread viruses infect application programs—spreadsheets, word processors, games, and utilities. When these programs are executed, a good virus will spread to other hosts.

Other viruses have more serious missions. The worst ones usually cause system crashes that result in lost data. But even more insidious is a new generation of viruses that modifies data without destroying it. Here's how one such virus performs:

Once a minute, it scans the computer screen. If it sees four numbers in a row, it transposes them in some fashion. You'll soon be refinancing your mortgage or replotting a CAM design using false data.

A Soviet virus called Black Hole wastes processor time by performing meaningless operations. It also makes a dark spot in one corner of the screen, thus the name.

In order to utilize or protect yourself from these programs, it's good to know what each type of virus really consists of.

First of all, when files are infected, a virus can move in several ways:

1) Simple mechanical copying of the virus code to clean files into the hard drive or other drives. This gives the virus more leverage in a user's software programming.

2) Shifting of virus-infected files through modem lines, thus sending the virus into the public domain or onto numerous bulletin boards. Virus files also move into LANs.

3) The physical reproduction of infected files by an operator.

In many instances a virus is installed by initializing the disk, locating the virus in the memory, changing it to the predefined memory area, admitting system information, and transferring the initial header back to the primary memory.

The similarities between a computer virus and a biological virus are quite evident. A lot of the things that are true about biological viruses (how they work and how to keep yourself clean from them) carry over to computer viruses, too.

A true virus is a program in itself. That is, it is an Executable Code which runs on a computer. More specifically, it's a set of instructions with two attributes: 1) it automatically reproduces itself, and (2) it causes another machine or program to do that reproduction.

Sounds simple? It is in some respects, but the effects can be anything but simple.

Whether it is RAM or disks or CD-Roms, memory is expensive. Any program that reproduces itself is bad because it uses memory, and memory is money. That's the heart of the problem with computer viruses.

By now, the term "computer virus" has come to stand for any kind of negative program. To a certain extent this is true for no other reason than its mass acceptance.

Note the names of some of the different types of viruses: worm, Trojan horse, time bomb, virus. Once one understands the analogies, they appear to be well named.

Trojan horses are probably the most famous and the most common form of infection, especially for revenge types. A Trojan horse virus, like the ancient trick, deals with a code embedded in or attached to another program. The user only knows about the "real" program and doesn't realize that when he runs it, this hidden program is going to do things he doesn't want it to do.

That's a Trojan horse.

True viruses spread automatically, which makes them different from Trojan horses. A Trojan horse program removes what is on a drive, but a virus affixes itself to regular applications or disks, making them carriers.

Caution should be used so the virus will infect only one file at a time to limit the original file's run count. This helps the virus remain undetected when the user operates.

A properly infected program can be used many times with no obvious problems except it will copy the virus section and attach to other disks/applications. When the final counter is reached, the virus will attack the disk itself.

A logic bomb is something that "explodes." It is usually a Trojan horse that goes off after a certain logical event. Disgruntled employees may create a logic bomb that keeps looking at employee records.

The most common virus is a special kind of logic bomb called a "time bomb." They are supposed to go off on Friday the 13th or the anniversary of some special event. One may find time bombs built into programs that came directly from the software manufacturer.

In essence, this insures that the developer gets paid. They buy a program with a time bomb in it. If they don't give you incentive to diffuse it (i.e., they don't pay you on time), the bomb will go off.

Bombs or hidden messages can even be found in hardware. Apple IIc computers have the names of the programmers embedded in their ROM. A simple three-line BASIC program will pull them up:

-IN#5

-INPUT A$

-Print A$

Hi, Dick, Hi Richard . . .

The two gentlemen who started Apple supposedly inserted a bomb in the design of the Macintosh that would cause a small figure to run across the screen and leave a message every 10,000th time the computer was turned on. Just to keep users in the correct frame of mind.

They were talked out of including it in the Mac.

Next in line are worms. A worm is a code stuck in another code. It's not like a Trojan horse, where you think you are running Lotus and it does something funny. A worm is its own program. It really only works on networks or boards. A good worm disguises itself as an authorized user, dives in, uses the system, and then zips away.

If a worm is given access to a network, it can do damn near anything to the host computer. The worm pretends it's an exec of the company that owns the computer, and the network has no reason to disbelieve it.

The worm goes, "I'm one of your VPs and I forgot the accounts receivable. Could you make me a copy of that?" It will send him a copy of the file. "I also need to delete these customers."

A worm has to pierce through any initial security measures. Once it does that, it has entered a computer system that it probably knows very little about, so it has to have the intelligence to discover enough about the system to move around and make the system do what you want it to do.

Then a worm can perform its mission: steal or copy certain files, crash things, maybe infect certain application programs. Whatever its task in life is . . .

Really good worms do one or two additional things.

It's probably going to want to gather up its data and erase all traces of its existence, then disappear. It may want to dissolve itself in order to cover the evidence that it was ever there, making the damage very difficult to find and repair.

Really, really good worms try to replicate and travel to other systems. If it captures passwords and phone numbers, it can try to dial those computers and masquerade as the computer that it is currently infecting.

A worm can be a major tool for revenge. It will sit in the computer for awhile and eat itself into the part where passwords are coming by, then grab the ones a user will need to mess up any files he wants to.

HOW DO PEOPLE CONSTRUCT A VIRUS?

WARNING! *This is for information purposes only!* Courts have held people liable for huge damages for passing on infected disks. Software producers and retail stores have been found legally responsible, too, even if they were not aware that the program was infected!

The author and the publisher of this book are not responsible for the use or misuse of the information herein, nor do we suggest in any way that a reader infect programs or computers!

Trojan horses normally feature a main program procedure that the user is accustomed to. Remember, a program is a set of instructions that will be complied and then executed (run) one at a time. Open this file, write to this file, read this file, take some input from the operator, etc.

A good Trojan horse will take the first instruction and tell the computer, "Before you do all those other things, I've got a couple tasks I'd like you to do. First let's erase everything on this hard disk . . ."

In order to hide the horse, it's usually placed at the bottom of the list of instructions. The first instruction will be a jump, causing the program to execute at the bottom first, where this Trojan horse is hiding. Then it returns to the normal run of the program.

A Trojan horse can either add to a file size or write over a section of the code that's already programmed. To be successful, it should pick a section that's almost never used so legitimate users won't notice it.

The first item in a Trojan horse is normally a "host identifier." The virus must decide whether to attack a particular program, so it has to somehow identify the program it wants to attack to find out whether it has already infected the program it is currently considering.

Some viruses don't look to see whether they have already infected a program, so they keep adding themselves to the back of the program over and over. Soon the virus program will take over the whole memory. These are easy to detect and stop before they complete their program.

After the host identifier comes a "trigger checker." This is either a time checker, logic checker, or a certain key stroke or operation that causes the virus to go off.

Then comes the infector, the actual impact device.

I have watched a low-level programmer write a boot infector virus in seventeen lines of code. His virus leapt onto the computer's boot program from a system disk before the rest

123

of the system could be activated.

It waited until the operator struck a particular key, locked up the keyboard, printed the words "Chaos is here," and then wiped out any disk connected to the computer.

How does an noncomputer person get his sweaty hands on a virus? Have a friendly programmer write one up for you, go through a bulletin board, or purchase a commercially available disk with a virus already included in the program.

It is then a simple matter to transfer it to any other disk (especially operating systems) and infect target computers.

A virus should be written in assembly language, "C," or any other that permits low-level functions. The following is a general list of steps my friend's virus used to accomplish its deadly task:

1) Open file.

2) Install first file into a main buffer.

3) Take first portion and save to alternate buffer.

4) Compute viral emplacement in new file: Viral Addr. = Application. Start. Addr. + Length of Application = 6.

5) Reserve a JUMP Viral Addr. at start of file.

6) Rewrite main buffer.

7) Set file pointer to tail of the file.

8) Write the alt. buff.

9) Write the viral code afterwards.

10) Shut the candidate file.

A virus could then destroy stuff by locking out the keyboard and resetting the keys. Or it can erase target data by finding all disk devices, wiping out the directory of each device, eliminating the key block for every file in the directory block, doing graphics or music, and presenting a text message. Then it can return to Application. Start. Addr. and work as if nothing has changed.

There are three places to plant viruses. One of the all-around best shots is at the beginning of every disk, called the boot sector. When a computer turns itself on, it doesn't know what it is or what to do—it's just a bunch of hardware. You have to have something to tell it, such as "go to the disk and pick up the program right at the beginning." That's called a boot program. If you infect that with a virus, there's no way that the computer will fail to execute it . . .

The problem with the boot program is that it is very short. It normally just loads in the operating system and goes away, so you are limited to a very small virus.

Today's more complicated viruses are usually system infectors.

Every computer has an operating system. It's called DOS, VAX, CBM, or whatever.

The operating system tells the computer how it writes things to the disk, how it picks things up from the keyboard, and how it displays things on the terminal. If you can infect that, it doesn't matter what program is run next. The infected operating system is now part of the way the computer thinks it's supposed to run.

Application infectors don't infect the operating system. They infect a single program. For example, if you know a person uses Lotus for his important functions, you can infect it so when it writes a file, it's going to want make a small error, or lose some data, or crash things.

Commercial software isn't always free from infection. A little while ago, Aldus Corporation released several thousand copies of Freehand, a graphics program, that contained a virus. In theory, a consultant hired by Aldus had picked up the virus from a computer game without ever realizing it. The beast was passed along to Freehand. Several other viruses have also found their way onto store shelves.

Unscrupulous stores and software manufacturers are at great risk, because even the rumor of infected programs being sold from one retail chain or from one manufacturer will pass quickly through the computer underground and can cause major damage to sales.

Viruses have been introduced in the past by a person purchasing computer software and then carefully, with a double-edged razor blade, slicing down one side of the plastic wrapping. The plastic is then gently removed from the box and saved. The product is taken out of the box and copies are made, or a small virus is inserted. The disk can now be placed back in the box, the plastic carefully refitted, and a small razor-cut strip of Scotch tape used to reseal it to nearly perfect specifications.

The software is then returned to the store under a variety of return clauses; you were simply not satisfied with the product, it did not live up to the manufacturer's specifications, or it was defective.

If you claim the item was defective, they will probably offer you another program in order to make up for the discrepancy.

If this happens, and one is really serious about revenge, it is possible to infect that program and then return it to another branch of the same store, assuming it's a retail chain.

Use the same story at the new store. This way it will appear that the company is manufacturing infected programs, since it will be discovered that this virus is available at a number of locations.

Nothing scares potential customers of computer programs as much the possibility that they could contain a virus.

REACH OUT AND TOUCH SOMEONE: COMMUNICATIONS REVENGE

Communications revenge comes in several different guises. Computer fraud and telephone fraud are two major areas in which phreaks and revengists get even with businesses. Best estimates—and they are just that, estimates—set these types of losses at around $4 billion a year.

How do these revenge schemes work? One way is the outside threat, where someone hacks into the computer via modem, steals or changes information, or steals money by manipulating the company's financial records.

However, the biggest threat comes from the guy who's actually authorized to be in the computer. He decides, "I want a big raise," or "I want this company to regret firing me."

Our insider simply sits down at the computer and grants his own wishes.

In today's business world, information is money. Information stolen out of computers can literally cripple a company. The federal government spends billions of dollars protecting information.

Many huge corporations spend megabucks protecting their main computer system, yet the most crucial information in that company is kept in a PC in the president's office, and it's totally unprotected. Companies like this are very vulnerable to information theft that can really hurt them.

Just as great a threat, from our vantage point, is that someone with quick access to a computer can change information rather than steal it. This change may go unnoticed for months, destroying the company's reputation and costing it business.

The thinking of late has been for companies to protect important computer modems off-line by inserting a human operator into the system. "In order to protect our computer, you have to go through our phone system to get to it. The operator has to connect you. We're safe," is the way the logic runs.

This is supposed to protect the info stored in the computer's files and prevent the unauthorized use of 800 (WATS) extensions by phreaks.

But does it really work?

"I'm Mark Tunafish with XXX TelCo and we're trying to repair the phone system. I need access to an outside line," is one method of social engineering one's way through the human portion of a PBX system.

The telephone system, in most cases, is far more vulnerable than the computer. Telephone fraud in this country is estimated to be somewhere around $700 million a year.

How does it happen? It's quite simple. Revenge folk and hackers have learned that the new phone systems have some real serious vulnerabilities.

Look at the easiest examples, PBXs, the large phone systems that serve a hundred or more offices in a company. Almost all of them have two things in common.

One is they have remote-access programming. That means they have a modem board built into them, so you call in on a phone line and get into the programming of that system.

The other common black hole is DICA, or "direct inward call access." DICA allows any executive to sit at home day or night, call his office, and get a tone back. Then he will enter a code. Once he has entered the code, the system dial tone comes back to him as if he were sitting at his desk and had just picked up his phone.

Our exec can do anything he can do from his office, including making long-distance phone calls. The DICA support has no toll restriction because it's designed for the private use of the top execs in the company.

This type of system is a major perk for the big executives, and sometimes it's used by salespeople on the road to control billing or control costs.

Inherent holes are built into these DICA systems, even if the DICA feature is not activated.

One gentleman I know offended a customer quite severely. The customer thought about it and then decided to apply some minimal hacking skills to crack his friend's DICA code.

128

One month later the exec was in a state of what could be referred to as total panic. He had just gotten his phone bill for $349,000.

He appealed to those friendly folk down at his phone company and they said, "You made them, you pay them. We don't care about the circumstances."

Many people think you can get out of those bills. *You cannot.* Some telephone companies may adjust them downward slightly, and they may give you prolonged periods to pay them off, but you *will* pay them or they will pull your phone lines.

One may have MCI, Sprint, or any other long-distance company, but remember; a Bell operating company owns those wires from your office to the long-distance carrier. They really don't have to worry about payments because they are the only game in town, and they *will* come take their wires back if necessary . . .

The company that had the $349,000 zapped to them had DICA in their system but never activated it. So how did our friendly phreak do it? Simple enough . . .

He broke into the remote access programming with a modem, followed the instructions in the system's operating manual (commercially available), programmed DICA to be active, and programmed in all his own access codes.

He left this information on a bunch of bulletin boards and put them on the phone company loops, telling people to help themselves. Many of the calls were to illegal numbers and telephone booths. The majority were to South America, Pakistan, and India.

Think these people are going to help some American corporation try to trace phone calls? Most Third World countries have better things to do with their little security forces than help AT&T.

The easiest way to hack DICA codes involves one glaring fact that remains true to this day. No matter who makes the equipment—Siemans, Mitell, Rolm, AT&T—every unit that leaves their plant *has the same security code in it.*

Every one of them. Each unit has an identical access code. Why? So it's easy for the installer to get into and program it during installation.

Do installers change them? No. Why should they? Unless the company is hip enough to demand that they be changed, they will remain factory-set throughout their lives. And these codes are in the manuals.

That's just one example of how to attack a corporation through its data/communication facilities.

A big secret: you know those automated answering computers in some offices that answer the phone with a recording, such as, "Please hold. All personnel are busy. If you know the extension number of the person you are trying to reach, dial it now."

Many of these systems have a backdoor trap. If you hit them with the correct Hz tone, it will cause them to trip and give you the system dial tone.

Once you are on the system dial tone, dial 8 and you will have a long-distance trunk. Most systems have nothing to stop anyone at this point because when you trip the system in this manner, it provides the highest rate of priority.

No toll restrictions.

Other ACDs (automatic call directing) have the same problem. There are several brands in use today that can be hit with a thousand-Hz tone burst as soon as they answer. Suddenly, "click," you're right into the system dial tone. Make your call back out of their system and they'll eat the bill.

Tones? Easy. Purchase a cheap AF generator from any electronics supply house or go directly through your computer. Most computers with sound capability can give you any frequency with one line of BASIC code.

If you can't write BASIC, there are cheap programs (even shareware) that will do this for you.

It's a short step to having your modem and computer dial and redial these numbers, trying different tones until a dial tone is discovered.

Another recent discovery that often works is to involve the operator. In order to make a call, say, overseas, two people share the same phone booth.

The caller gives the operator the number for an automated attendant system—an in-house system that handles incoming calls—and says he needs to reach a Steve Smith. The operator leaves the caller on the circuit while she calls to verify the authorization to make the call.

The automated attendant answers and says, "Hold for Mr. Smith." Our trickster reaches up and hits a 1 on the phone touch pad. The operator can't tell where the tone came from, but the tone is heard by the automated attendant and it goes off-line.

The phone is then grabbed by the second man in the booth and he says, "Hello, this is Mr. Smith. I authorize the call." Guess who's going to get the bill?

How do people get into computers at a target company? Many companies, because of the way they operate, cannot shut their modem down for one minute in any 24-hour period. That computer has to be on 24 hours a day, seven days a week.

This gives lots of uncrowded time for people to try to hack codes and passwords.

Numbers can be found by simply dialing around the company's main phone numbers until a modem answers, or they can be socially engineered out of an employee or obtained by Dumpster diving.

If you have physical contact with a PC, it's pretty easy to beat passwords on many systems. If it's an IBM or one of the IBM clones and it's MS-DOS based, one can enter that computer while it is booting up and get all the way around security codes by hitting two specific keys at the same time while it's booting (the keys vary, depending on the DOS).

It's that simple.

You also can take one of your own floppy disks with DOS loaded on it, load it into the target computer, and defeat whatever protection was on the original DOS program simply by replacing it with your new one.

How do you get into the president's office to get to his PC? By becoming invisible. Few people question telephone repair people, workmen, carpet installers, and so on.

Question them? Few people ever even notice them.

One of the most best ways to gain access is through the cleaning crew. They've got to go in and empty the trash can in the president's office. The average cleaning person makes four- to five-dollars per hour. They can be bribed, or it's pretty easy to lie and get a job in the actual crew . . .

How easy is it to get information out of an executive's PC? Once you're in, it's a piece of cake. If you're on a cleaning crew, you go in, pull up the files you want, copy them onto a disk, pop the disk out, stick it in something, and walk.

Computer revenge tricks can be accomplished in several areas:

Once someone is in the computer, be it an employee or someone from the outside, they can hurt the company by stealing information or putting in a virus. Either can be disastrous to a company.

The intruder can simply manipulate and change information instead of taking files. Why? It's possible to change a financial report to make the company look like shit, or erase part of a customer list, cutting the business off at the neck, or just scramble the billing process.

Thieves also break into computers for the sole purpose of finding purchase order or credit card numbers in order to abuse a company's credit.

Although telephone and computer fraud is illegal, only a very few cases are ever prosecuted. If a bank gets tapped for a half a million dollars or a big company gets hit for a couple hundred thousand, do they run to the media and say, "Let me tell you what happened to us . . ."?

No. They keep it secret. In many cases, they won't even report it to the proper law enforcement agencies.

They know if the scam becomes public, it will damage stockholders' confidence in the company and hurt its public image. Companies, especially public ones, are very sensitive to both these things, so most crimes go unreported.

BULLETIN BOARDS

In today's world of electronic communications, the hacker phreak or revenge artist is never alone. Help is only as far away as your telephone, or more correctly, as far away as your modem. Reach out and touch someone.

One way to solicit ideas, get technical help, and distribute gleaned information, including phone numbers of people who have done horrendous things and need some moral punishment from the community at large, is from bulletin boards. You may already belong to a bulletin board, such as CompuServe, Dialog, Orpheus, or any other large, public board.

Bulletin boards are the electronic equivalent of the originals that grace the walls of stores and hallways. If someone desires information, they post a notice. Others answer and give the information desired.

The electronic bulletin board operates in a new way. Answers can be nearly instantaneous as users of the bulletin board begin posting live return mail from everywhere in the country.

What is an electronic bulletin board? Like any other computer operation, it is a program that operates from a computer. It works with a modem to present verified operators with a format for giving their opinions, data, and solicitations, as well as providing information on how to reply to calls. Most bulletin boards have at least one public area where anyone may expound on nearly anything.

Bulletin boards can offer facilities that permit a user to send announcements to another user, called E-mail or electronic mail. Such messages can range from information about used car parts to where a party is in progress.

On most boards you will discover an area of special interest groups (SIGS), and usually there will be a hackers' club or techie club. The owner of the group will decide who may enter his area. Since the bulletin board's software permits the system operator to hide the list of SIGs from other users, it may not be apparent whether a hackers' section exists on a board until later. The sysop may desire to view a new person before allowing him to a "sensitive" area. Some bulletin boards even carry two hacker sections; one is easy to get into while the second is a tightly controlled secret, allowing only highly trusted users to exchange data.

The first timer, looking through a hackers' bulletin board, will discover that it appears to be a group of conversations between friends. A person may write up a summary for public access. Questions will be asked. Any other member can answer, since the idea is to exchange information.

Always bear in mind that though you think you are communicating directly with another person and only that person, there are some limits to that security. The system operator—the person who set the system up, physically maintains it, and has control of the program—has access to *everything* that goes through the bulletin board, no matter if it's confidential, conference format, or left in an individual's "private" mailbox. The system operator can view anything at his discretion, as well as eliminate or modify everything on the board.

One should also bear in mind that the FBI likes to infiltrate bulletin boards and has one department that does nothing but that. There is also a rather infamous private detective in the state of Oregon who makes a living out of infiltrating bulletin boards and turning people over to the correct law enforcement agencies.

Rumor claims that the FBI actually operates a couple of boards in order to keep up with the rapidly changing techniques that travel through the computer community, as well as to track and possibly arrest hackers.

Then there's the problem of rollovers. A number of ex-hackers and phreaks, even some of the "top" names in the national bulletin-board hierarchy, have seen the error of their ways (usually encouraged by a visit or two from the FBI) and now work for the forces of law and order. There's a small company on the East Coast operated by several ex-phreaks who work through bulletin boards to make sure there's no damaging information on them with regards to your company or private life. They also help officials in law enforcement get on bulletin boards by using their old hacker names as references.

What I'm trying to say here is that, in my opinion, it is foolish to commit or solicit illegal acts on a bulletin board. If you want to pass sensitive information, you should be certain of the person you're passing it to and *not* do it through a bulletin board.

Most bulletin boards operate in levels. The first level is available to anyone allowed to join. The second level is the sensitive level, where confidential/hacking/phreaking information is passed, such as how to get in companies, how to mess up files, how to plant various bombs, etc. It usually requires a waiting period to become accepted into this level, and during that period you are usually expected to contribute something valuable to the other players, such as phone numbers, passwords, or at least several references to other known and therefore "safe" hackers.

Many bulletin boards will actually send you an application form on which you list the other hackers who you want to use for verifying your reliability. *They will check on these references.*

Be aware that once you've given your phone number on a bulletin board, that phone number is listed for months or even years and will travel to other bulletin boards. You can expect calls at all times of the day or night from people who are not necessarily paying for the calls and don't have a lot to lose. If you get a reputation as a narc or a crasher or something worse, you can expect electronic retribution to swiftly follow.

Most revengists find that reaching the second level of a bulletin board is sufficient to complete their projects. In order to go beyond this level and join the third, secret level, most system operators require personal contact or at least getting to know enough about you that they can verify your identity or reasons for progressing. Many bulletin board members do not realize this third level even exists.

Bulletin boards are fun. You can make contact with all sorts of creative people who will suggest all sorts of interesting things, often find out tricks for getting around security blocks and ideas for almost anything in the world, from revenge to good recipes and other generally interesting stuff. You'll also find it runs your phone bill up in a bloody hurry.

How do you find bulletin boards? The accepted manner is to read your local computer newspapers and buy the national computer magazines. *Computer Shopper* is one of the better national publications that lists bulletin boards by the hundreds, including their interests and additional pieces of information.

Computer clubs, meetings, or LANS (Local Area Networks) are other fertile grounds for prying out elusive bulletin board numbers. For those of you who believe capitalism triumphs over all, there's an instant way to find over 10,000 active bulletin boards from every part of the

United States! It's Ed Gelb's Instant Bulletin Board Phone Directory Baud Database (database phone number: 201-694-6835).

Ed operates a continuous bulletin board for bulletin boards. When you call, 24-hours a day, you get information on how to join his bulletin board. This requires a small payment from a credit card, or you can get an address to which to mail in payment (I believe it's about ten dollars as of this writing). This gives you two hundred minutes of access to his bulletin board. You can buy more increments in one-hundred-minute blocks for the same price.

What's on it? More than 10,000 bulletin boards located by state or, if they are in Canada, province. Ed verifies his listings on a continuing basis.

This service is easy to use. It features a help menu that tells you how to get into the bulletin boards, or you can request a list of boards in a certain area and his system will search them out for you. It's easy to navigate Ed's instructions and download the information so you can get lists and lists and lists of bulletin boards. It is definitely a good place to begin if you are interested in pursuing this hobby.

As Ed says, if a bulletin board is not on his list, it's not worth calling . . .

ESD:
ELECTROSTATIC DISCHARGE

Nikola Tesla was a man well known for his research into DC, pulsed DC, and high-frequency electricity. His experiments could transmit electricity directly through the earth for many miles so effectively that people could tap the power simply by going to ground. He developed devices that could produce two-hundred-foot lightning bolts, and others that could light streetlights twenty-five miles from the source *without wires*.

One of his inventions makes an appearance in every junior high school science fair in the world. It is known as the Tesla coil. It collects high-frequency, high-voltage energy that acts quite unlike conventional electricity. It does not stop at most insulation.

High-frequency voltage will transmit its energy through the air without wires as well as produce heat and lightning-like light. Yet it will pass through human tissue with virtually no feeling or shocking effects.

Tesla coils are often seen in old science fiction movies or comedies where the protagonist touches the coil and his hair stands on end, or he holds a fluorescent light bulb in one hand and touches the coil and the bulb lights up. The high-frequency current passes through tissue with virtually no damage.

There are, however, some materials it will not pass through without harm, such as electrical circuits . . .

A friend of mine, an electronics engineer, made a startling discovery one day. As with many great discoveries, he did it purely by accident.

My friend was working on a medium-power, tabletop Tesla coil. He turned it on without thinking. In the next second or so it wiped out the entire contents of his hard disk, his answering machine, and, *through a wall*, a credit card he had sitting on a table about ten feet away. *And the computer and answering machine were not even plugged in!*

Just picture the damage that could be caused by the use of this device in environments with home computers as well as small and large businesses.

Good coils are available from Information Unlimited, among other sources. (See the Suppliers chapter for addresses.)

Be very, very careful when using a Tesla coil around any electrical equipment.

STUN GUNS

Most people are familiar with electronic stun guns, such as those made by Nova Technologies, designed to freeze an antagonist's muscles by the use of high-frequency, pulsing current. These devices are carried by security guards, cops, women, and occasionally by people who simply like to see other people's muscles freeze and watch them drop to the ground in writhing agony for a couple of minutes.

There's another group of users for these guns because, you see, they also put out our old buddy, ESD. That's right, these are electrostatic discharge devices. The common ones put out 65,000 volts. The trick is to get one of the new generation units, which put out *120,000* volts. These are available from a variety of suppliers, including Omega and Information Unlimited.

What can you do with 120,000 volts of high-frequency electricity? The obvious use is that you can put anyone on the ground for a couple of minutes. The units do that very effectively.

Imagine being kicked by a very angry mule and you'll have some idea of what it feels like to be on the receiving end of a powerful stun gun.

Most stun guns have two paths for the voltage to travel. The first consists of two bent electrodes that aim toward each other. These provide a route through the ether so the device will operate when you press the discharge button. This lightning-like display tends to discourage all animals and most humans with an IQ of over three from approaching you any further.

The second path consists of a second pair of electrodes that are simply straight pins set further apart than the bent ones. When the straight pins contact anything that can transmit electricity, they become the path of least resistance, directing the flow of electricity through them. This works quite well because air gaps are a fairly high source of resistance.

On the label:

DANGER

HIGH VOLTAGE

HANDLE AND USE THIS DEVICE AS YOU WOULD ANY WEAPON, with care and caution. You, as the owner user of this unit, assume all liabilities for any damages and/or bodily injury which may occur. It is the owner's/user's responsibility to comply with Local, State and Federal regulations, if any, that may pertain to the ownership of this product or its use.

DO NOT discharge the unit during testing for more than ½ second at a time. DUE TO THE HIGH VOLTAGE continuous discharge can damage the unit & void your warranty.

120 KV

120K zapper. A high-frequency electrostatic discharge device that will drop muggers, freeze animals, zap silicon chips, wipe out computerized data, reset alarms, and generally give the average person a few of Superman's powers. This model produces approximately twice the voltage of a standard stun gun.

Stun guns can be modified slightly by placing plastic tape or pencil erasers over the bent electrodes, thereby canceling them as a path of the discharge, leaving only the straight "contact" electrodes in effect.

This will heighten the reaction to some stun guns by closing off the air path, which may leak part of the charge. More importantly, one can now run wires from the straight electrodes to anything one desires and electrify it.

Remember, the target must complete the circuit in order to feel the shock, so the wires have to go to two separate, preferably metal items in the same vicinity, such as a welcome mat and a doorknob, car handle and button, dead bolt and doorknob, or virtually anything that will be grasped, thus completing the circuit.

Most of these stun guns can have their on/off switches taped in the "on" position. Once someone completes the circuit with his body, the guns will discharge their full effect into the highest point of resistance.

This being the victim.

When properly executed, this trick is amazing. You don't know the feelings that go through your body and mind when you've grabbed 120,000 volts without knowing it's there.

Until you've done it.

It's possible that some stun guns will not retain their full voltage over long periods of time, as they may leak between the devices you've now designated as electrodes, depending on what the resistance is between them.

More in line with our thoughts, heavy doses of electrostatic electricity will do interesting things to electronic devices. For instance, the discharge of this unit can perform, but is not limited to, some of the following applications:

1) Zap floppy disks. The discharge will scramble the information beyond retrieval.

2) Zap hard disks. If the disk is not grounded correctly or sometimes even if it is, ESD will irretrievably damage the data and formatting on the disk.

3) Zap chips! Yes, most modern chips, especially CMOS or other surface-technology

140

chips, cannot take static discharges. They will burn out if a 120,000-volt unit is discharged near a computer board, video equipment, television set, modem, or just about any other type of electronic equipment. It will zap the chip, burning it out.

4) Do freaky things to an alarm system. If there is a keypad, key, or button-setting system on the outside of a building, zap it with your stun gun and see what happens. Some systems will automatically reset and go into the alarm mode, then will be set off the first time someone inside moves past the sensor or opens the door. If the alarm is already set, the gun may cause it to go off immediately without leaving any visible footprints of how it was done.

Be gentle with your stun gun. It will ruin electronic gear beyond recognition and make a real dent in your social life if you don't resist the temptation to zap your friends every time they say something insulting.

CAPACITORS: THE SHOCKING TRUTH

The lowly capacitor is another device that is fully charged (excuse the pun) with potential. Capacitors are devices that store charges of electricity. Once charged, a good tubular capacitor will stay hot for an hour or two before the electricity gradually leaks into the atmosphere.

Capacitors vary in the amount of charge they will hold by their size and rating. Good-sized capacitors can be purchased for under one dollar at your friendly Radio Shack store, or you can simply get an automotive capacitor from an automobile supply house.

Capacitors may be used in a number of ways. First, they have to be charged. If it's a two-wire capacitor, observe the polarity markings, if any.

If it's an automotive capacitor, you must bear in mind that the metal sleeve of the capacitor is one pole and the wire is the other. Capacitors can be charged from fairly high-voltage sources, such as a car ignition system, by simply connecting the capacitor to the high-voltage side of the coil or even to a spark plug wire, or they can be charged by a device especially designed for charging capacitors.

The latter suggestion is both safer and easier.

In a pinch, they can even be charged off an AC power line, *but only if one knows what one is doing.* Do not fool around with AC power or, for that matter, high voltage from any source without a grasp of the principles of electricity. Getting hit with 120 volts is not fun.

I speak from experience . . .

Once a capacitor is charged, the possibilities for its use are multifold. A friend of mine used to charge a good-size capacitor and then bend the two leads using a wooden pencil so they were on the opposite sides of the capacitor.

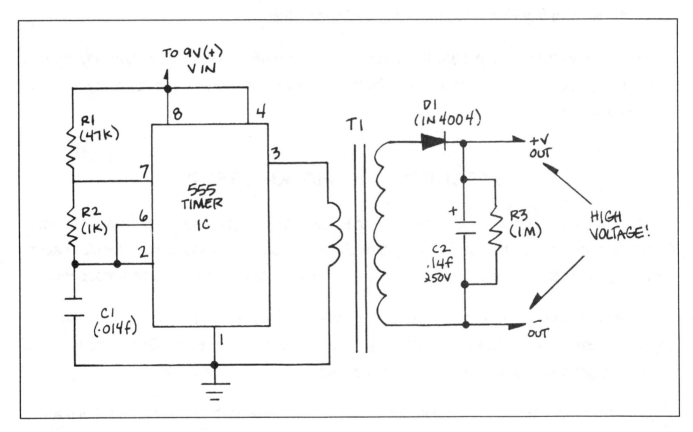

Circuit page for a high-voltage shocker and capacitor charger.
T1: miniature 6.3V:120V power transformer (RS 273-1384 or similar);
R1: 47K resistor; R2: 1K resistor; C1: .01 mf; C2: .1 uf, 250V;
R3: 1M resistor; D1: 1N4004, power supply: +5 to 9V (V in).

He would then delight in calling to somebody, "Here," and throwing the capacitor in his direction. The natural reaction is to catch the damn thing, which brings the target in contact with both wires, rather abruptly delivering a healthy shock.

His next best move was to place the same charged unit inside an open book. When the

142

owner came to pick up the book, he'd close it, shorting the capacitor out and delivering a miniature blast of lightning. Please note that in one instance it set the book on fire, causing a rather larger disturbance than my friend had intended.

A really, really mean thing to do with a capacitor is to run very thin wires or conductive paint across a toilet seat. Hide the capacitor out of sight and when someone sits down . . .

An even meaner, meaner thing to do is to build the device shown in the diagram from a few Radio Shack parts and use it as a source of high voltage. In this case, you don't need to charge a capacitor. This circuit is a constant source of high-voltage pulses. Some ruthless people have gone a step farther than the previous trick by placing an aluminum foil bath mat in front of the toilet and running one wire into the bowl.

If a person were to step on the conductive mat in his bare feet or with nonrubber-soled shoes and urinate into the bowl, a circuit would suddenly be closed between the high voltage source, the person, and the conductive stream of . . .

This is a nonsexist device. It works equally well on standers or sitters and, man, it is an experience that people will never forget.

The device is extremely simple to make and extremely inexpensive, which is important in this instance, because if the shockee finds it afterwards, he/she is going to smash it into extremely small bits.

Again, I speak from the rude side of experience.

With a little application of imaginative cross-thinking, this device can also be used to electrify car door handles, steering wheels, common household appliances, or other available, usually inert objects, to help return someone's personality, not to mention his sense of right and wrong . . .

MAGNETIC FORCE

A few years ago, magnets were thought of by revengists as a simple child's toy good for only minor tricks to amuse and irritate an audience. Today we realize that they can be a major threat to various types of technology.

Almost all of today's data is stored on some sort of magnetic media. Videotapes, audio-tapes, floppy disks, and computer tapes are all electronically stored, magnetically affectable data mediums.

If any of these items are exposed to a magnetic field, especially a changing magnetic field of enough strength, the information on the media will realign itself with the new magnetic lines of force, permanently wiping out any information stored on the media.

This means that a perpetrator with a powerful-enough magnet can simply approach a floppy disk or a tape, rub the magnet back and forth at close range, and instantly wipe out God knows how much data.

The variables in this formula are time, distance, and strength of field. The stronger the magnetic force, the farther away the magnet can be and still operate efficiently. The longer the data is exposed to the magnetic force, the more likely it is to realign with the new orders.

There are some extremely small but powerful magnets with unusually high energy output that were not available a few years ago. Rare earth cobalt magnets provide extreme power in a small package and can be obtained from most scientific-equipment suppliers.

Although not quite as strong, Alnico or Alcomax magnets are available almost anywhere in a number of shapes and sizes that make them cost- and revenge-effective.

Generally speaking, the higher the price of the magnet, the better it's going to be for revenge applications. Magnetic strength is measured in gauss, and obviously the higher the gauss the better the chance we have of utilizing it for our purposes.

Other times you'll notice magnets, especially electromagnets, that are listed in lifting power. A note here: we tested a $50, two-hundred-pound-pull electromagnet (this means it would legitimately lift two hundred pounds of steel when energized and applied to a flat, clean, steel plate) with high expectations, only to find that though the lifting force was extremely powerful, the force of field, the extended gauss, was not up to snuff.

Permanent rare earth cobalts and even Alnico magnets did a much better job of erasing, or rather rearranging, data on all types of media than did the rather expensive electromagnets. Electromagnets are fun to play with but are really not very good for our applications.

At what range can data be disoriented? With a strong, permanent rare earth cobalt magnet, we found that it's possible to muddy audiotapes and videotapes from a distance of one to two inches with a couple of back and forth sweeps of the magnet. As the time increases or the distance decreases, the signal on the tape will be erased for all time.

Floppy disks are affected in approximately the same manner. The formatting function falls out fairly fast at a distance of one-half to one inch with just a quick sweep. A bit of testing with a particular magnet and a particular type of test object will give you the exact measurements necessary for any covert operation you may want to undertake.

Bringing a magnet into contact with medium materials is easier than it sounds because magnetic lines of force cut through most inert (especially nonmetallic) materials as if they were not there. A magnet can be concealed in a sleeve, glove, pocket, shirt, pants, or in a thin briefcase, and the obstruction will prove no more serious than if it were a simple air gap. People have been known to use this fact to harass video and record stores that have given them trouble in the past. Others have wiped out data by approaching a secretary's desk, laying one's gloves, briefcase, or plastic sack on a disk or box of disks, and asking a question or two.

Remember, it's best to move the magnet back and forth a few times so the lines of force vary and realign the media in an incoherent fashion.

Because magnets come in all shapes and sizes, including flat, paper-thin formats and as flexible magnetic tape, they can be creatively cut or painted and placed in such interesting places as underneath a desk blotter, underneath a mouse pad, or, best of all, in the bottom of a floppy disk file. Because the thinness of these magnets restricts their strength, they don't work nearly as fast

May the force be with you. **A variety of magnets for a variety of uses. Note the subminiature models arranged around the circumference of the ceramic version. These minimagnets are the perfect size and shape for inclusion in a tape player, Walkman, VCR, or other magnetic media machine.**

as their more powerful cousins, but they will degrade data over a period of time.

One of the most creative tricks I've seen using magnetic force was a gentleman I know who makes a habit of fastening extremely small magnets with a drop of super glue right next to the heads in audio and videotape recorders. If it is positioned on the correct side of the head, it will allow the tape to be played once and then erase it immediately afterwards.

If the tape's speed is high or the tape is not quite in contact with the magnet, it can take more than one run, but the degeneration starts immediately. Most people never think to look for something like this. If they did notice it, the average person wouldn't realize that it was an add-on feature that didn't originally come with the tape deck.

Magnets of all strengths, sizes, and shapes can easily be purchased from scientific supply houses. Edmund Scientific Company (see Suppliers chapter) has one of the better selections we've seen.

UNIVERSAL PRODUCT CODES

Universal product codes, or as they are popularly called, bar codes, are made up of several parallel lines and a number under each code. The lines are of various widths and determine what a cash register reads as it goes over the code.

This labor-saving invention provides several chances for revenge. Prices can be altered for yourself or for the good of mankind. Either way will wreak havoc with the store . . .

The bar code must be clean, not greasy or covered with other markings, to be read automatically. If it is screwed up and cannot be scanned, the clerk must enter it by hand.

Bar codes are seen in various shapes, sizes, and hues. They are printed on bottles, cans, and most other containers. Sometimes they are printed on a peel-off label, which allows them to be switched around if the inclination suddenly appears to do so.

The computer signals that it has registered a code by making a beeping noise. *Store clerks seldom look at the price or the name of the item shown on the screen.*

If it beeps, it's gotta be okay . . .

Small address labels can be obtained from stationery outlets that are made for use in photocopy machines. Peel-off labels are manufactured in 8 1/2" x 11" sheets. With a good copy machine, one could manufacture bar labels at home.

For a hobby only, of course.

How?

Take some bar codes from actual products, lay them out on the sheets, photocopy, and *poof!*

Now go out and substitute bar codes. It is a simple matter to affix these over the store's original label.

And remember our motto:
Always be polite . . .